Antigua
& Barbuda

Don Philpott

Published in the UK by
Landmark Publishing Ltd,
Waterloo House, 12 Compton,
Ashbourne, Derbyshire DE6 1DA

Published in the USA by
Hunter Publishing Inc
130 Campus Drive, Edison NJ 08818

Don Philpott is a journalist, author and broadcaster who has spent the last thirty years exploring the world as a writer. Born in Hull, England, he worked for twenty years with the Press Association, the UK national news agency. He founded and co-edited *Footloose* an outdoor activities magazine in the UK.

Acknowledgment

My sincere thanks go to all the people who helped me with research and assistance while writing this book. In particular I would like to thank the Antigua and Barbuda Department of Tourism, especially Karen Knowles and Dawn Anthony; Sandals Antigua Resort and Spa, American A' '' Yepton Beach Resort and Roberta Gar

Dedication
To my American I

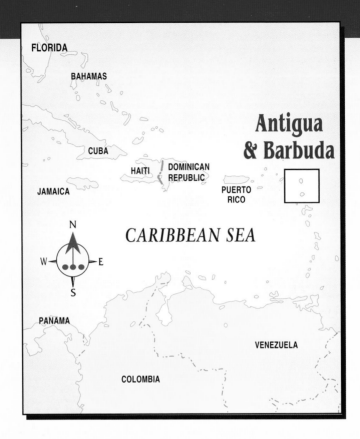

Antigua & Barbuda

FLORIDA

BAHAMAS

CUBA

HAITI   DOMINICAN REPUBLIC

JAMAICA

PUERTO RICO

N
W   E
S

CARIBBEAN SEA

PANAMA

VENEZUELA

COLOMBIA

Mamora Bay

CONTENTS

FACTFILE

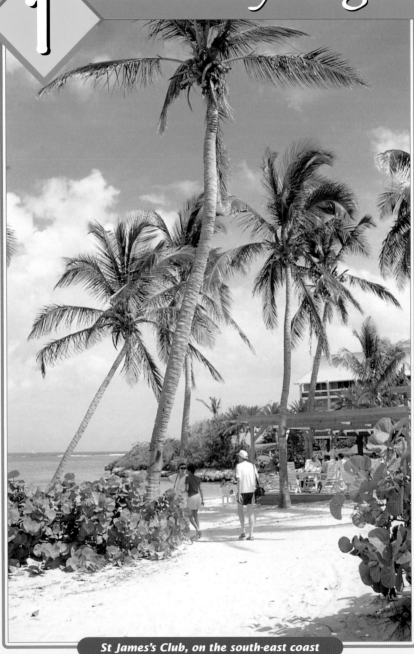

St James's Club, on the south-east coast

The twin island state of Antigua and Barbuda boasts some of the finest beaches in the Caribbean and superb year-round weather with high sunshine and low rainfall and humidity.

The waters offer world-class diving and sailing, and there is a wealth of other watersports. You can enjoy luxurious hotels and great restaurants – and some of the freshest seafood you will ever taste. There are duty-free boutiques and crafts markets, laid back beach bars, action-packed casinos, and historic sites and attractions. Above all, there is a warm and friendly people waiting to make your trip, one you will never forget.

Note: Antigua is pronounced as An-tee-gar.

When to Go

Many people feel that between November and April is the best time to visit because it is drier and cooler. Temperatures, however, do not vary a great deal throughout the year and any time is a good time to visit.

Getting there

By air

The VC Bird International Airport is 4 miles (6km) north-east of St John's, and is served by scheduled flights operated by a number of international carriers. There is a tourist information desk, duty-free shops, bank, post office, car rental agency, taxi rank, restaurant and two bars. Always agree the taxi fare beforehand. Typical fares are US$7 to St John's, and US$21 to both Shirley Heights and Nelson's Dockyard.

From Europe – British Airways flies direct from London Gatwick (8 hours). Virgin Atlantic have twice weekly direct flights. BWIA flies from London Heathrow and Zurich, and Condor flies from Frankfurt (9 hours). Air France flies weekly from Paris to Antigua (8 hours) and St Martin and are handled locally by LIAT although reservations have to be made in Guadeloupe ☎ 011-590-826211. There are also many charter flights during the summer. Many airlines fly to Miami and San Juan, Puerto Rico, where connecting flights can be taken to Antigua. Air France flies to Guadeloupe and KLM flies from Amsterdam to St Maarten, from where there are LIAT connections to Antigua.

From the US and Canada – Airline connections are offered by American Airlines through its Miami (3 hours) and San Juan hubs

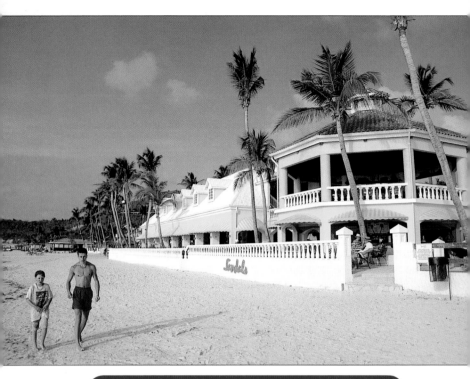

Above: Sandals Antigua Resort, north of St John's
Opposite: Antigua's resorts are all stunningly located

(1 hour). Air Canada flies from Toronto and BWIA flies from Miami, New York and Toronto. Continental Airlines flies from Newark and Baltimore (both 4 hours). There are also connecting flights via St Martin.

From the Caribbean – LIAT operates schedule services between Antigua and Anguilla, Barbados, Barbuda, Caracas, Carriacou, Dominican Republic, Dominica, Grenada, Guadeloupe, Guyana, Martinique, Montserrat, Nevis, Port of Spain, San Juan, St Lucia, St Maarten, St Thomas, St Vincent, Tortola and British Virgin Islands. Air St Kitts-Nevis, Carib Aviation, Montserrat Airways and Norman Aviation also operate from VC Bird International Airport, and offer charters to many islands close by.

By sea

St John's has two ports which serve visiting cruise ships – St John's Deep Water Harbour and the modern cruise ship facility at Heritage Quay. Cruise ships also visit Nelson's Dockyard in English Harbour. Each year more than 300 cruise ships visit Antigua, together with thousands of yachts. Official points of entry are St John's, St James's Club and Crabb's Marina.

Location and Landscape

The independent state of Antigua and Barbuda, together with their dependency of Redonda, lies in the north-eastern part of the Caribbean Sea and are part of the Leeward

Islands in the middle of the Lesser Antilles chain. To the west are the islands of Saba, St Eustatius, St Kitts and Nevis; to the south, the French island of Guadeloupe; and to the north, British Anguilla, French Saint Barthélemy and Dutch/French Sint Maarten/Saint Martin. Antigua is 295 miles (420km) south-south-east of Puerto Rico, and 1,300 miles (2,106 km) south-east of Miami.

The northern and eastern coasts of Antigua and Barbuda face the Atlantic Ocean, and the western and southern coasts face the Caribbean Sea.

Antigua

The island is 15 miles (24km) from east to west and 11 miles (18km) from north to the south at its widest. It covers 108 sq miles (280 sq km), and is the largest of the Leeward Islands. The island, consisting almost entirely of limestone coral, has a very indented coastline with many large deep-water bays and inlets offering safe anchorage, although the inshore waters off the north and north-east coasts can be treacherous due to reefs and shallows. The nature of the coastline gives rise to 365 sandy beaches, backed by gently rolling hills, often wooded or clad in lush flowering vegetation.

Lying on the edge of the Caribbean plate the island is volcanic in origin, and was literally pushed above the surface of the sea by the pressure on the plate rim. It is generally low-lying with the highest land in the south-west. Boggy

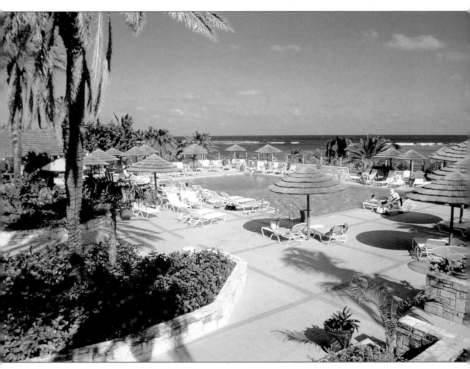

Peak at 1,330ft (405m) is the highest point. The island has no rivers and few springs, and the Potworks Dam Reservoir is the principal source of drinking water. The main town is St John's, the capital.

Barbuda

Originally called Dulcina, is 25 miles (40km) north of Antigua, 14 miles (23km) from east to west, and 9.6 miles (15km) from north to south and covers an area of 62 sq miles (160 sq km). It is a wooded coral island with low hills and teems with wildlife. The highest point is Lindsay Hill at 143ft (44m) above sea level. There are no rivers or lakes on the island and the rainfall is less than on Antigua. The main settlement is Codrington.

Redonda

An uninhabited island rock 34 miles (55km) south-west of Antigua. It rises out of the sea to a height of 1,000ft (305m) and covers an area of 0.6 sq miles (1.6 sq km).

History

Long before the Spaniards arrived, the islands had been settled by several different groups of Amerindians – Siboney (or Ciboney), Taino, Arawak and Caribs – who had passed through the Caribbean from South America. There is evidence of Amerindian Siboney settlements dating back to 2000BC. The name Siboney comes from the Arawak word for 'cave-dweller', although many also preferred to live in small settlements close to the coast. They were Stone Age hunters and gatherers, and fashioned rough tools and weapons from stones and shells.

From the time of Christ, Arawaks started to arrive from nearby Caribbean islands to the south to escape the warlike Carib Indians. They named the island Wadaldi.

The Arawaks

The Arawaks were a peaceful people who grew basic crops like suchas, maize, manioc and peppers. They also fished and foraged for food such as turtles and iguanas which were in plentiful supply. They lived in round, thatched 'hurricane-proof' huts in small villages ruled by a cacique (chieftain), and were skilled potters, weavers and boat builders. Their dug-out canoes were incredibly seaworthy, and their weaving skills were such that they could weave

Christopher Columbus

Antigua was 'discovered' by Christopher Columbus during his second voyage of exploration in 1493. He named the island after Santa Maria de la Antigua, the miracle-working patron saint of the cathedral in Seville, Spain, from whose port his expedition sailed. One of his three ships was named *Santa Maria*, the others being *Nina* and *Pinta*. After his death Columbus was buried in Seville Cathedral for a short time before being re-interred in the cathedral of Santo Domingo on Hispaniola.

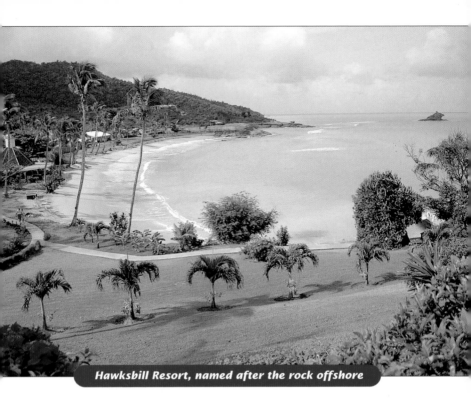

Hawksbill Resort, named after the rock offshore

baskets from strips of palms that were totally watertight. The Arawaks slept in beds slung between two poles, and the hammock is one of their legacies. They worshipped gods of nature, represented by statues or idols made of wood, stone or bone.

The Caribs

The Arawaks were followed by the Caribs, who were feared warriors. Their battle canoes were powered by a hundred or more paddles and could, over a short distance, overhaul a sailing ship.

The original name of the Caribs was Kalina, meaning 'we alone are people'. The Spanish confused this with their word 'cariba', which was short for 'caribales' meaning cannibal, and this was then shortened to carib.

The Caribs were feared by early European explorers because of horrific stories about cannibalism, with victims being roasted alive on spits. They were even reported to have a taste preference, thinking Frenchmen were the most tasty, followed by the English and the Dutch, with the Spanish considered stringy and almost inedible.

Villages were built inland in forest clearings and huts had timber walls and thatched roofs. Early paintings show that the Caribs enjoyed dancing, either for pleasure or as part of rituals, and they played ball games. They were primarily fishermen and hunters, although they did cultivate kitchen gardens and developed a system of shift cultivation, known as 'conuco'. They were also accomplished potters and weavers.

European occupation

The Spanish, having claimed ownership of the islands, then largely ignored them because of the hostile Indians and the lack of fresh water, and because there were much richer pickings further west on the islands of Cuba, Hispaniola and Puerto Rico.

Antigua was first settled by the English, from St Kitts, who landed in 1632 and claimed the island for the English crown. The settlers were attacked by the Caribs, but the Indians were no match against the well-armed English. The Caribs were either killed or enslaved or they fled, and the settlers cleared the land and planted tobacco, indigo and ginger. The island remained in English hands although numerous attempts were made to take it by other foreign powers, especially the French and Spanish. In 1666 the French occupied the island for six months.

Barbuda

Barbuda was not settled until 1678. Seven years later the British crown deeded the island to the Codrington family who used it to rear livestock and grow some cotton, the soil not being rich enough for sugar cane. There are many legends telling of the island's use as a slave farm, where the strongest, tallest slaves were used for breeding. It is possible that a slave farm was planned for Barbuda but there is no evidence that one ever existed, although some historians and anthropologists have suggested that it did, and this would account for the Barbudians being such a tall people.

Emancipation in 1834 hit the economy of the islands hard, and

Christopher Codrington

In 1674 Sir Christopher Codrington arrived on Antigua from Barbados and established the first large sugar plantation, which he named Betty's Hope after his daughter. Many of the plantation names ended in words such as 'Hope' which showed the settlers' optimism, while several plantations with the word 'Rest' in the name indicate that the owner or a member of his close family is buried on the property.

In the late 17th century most of the tobacco plantations had followed Codrington's example and switched to growing sugar cane, which yielded much higher profits. Huge areas of land were cleared and more than 150 sugar mills were built to process the crop. Many of these old mills still stand in varying states of disrepair.

It is said that in the mid-18th century, Antigua, because of its sugar, was considered more important to Britain than all the 13 North American colonies, Canada and India combined. The fortunes generated by sugar were so great that Antigua had to be heavily fortified, with about 40 gun emplacements, batteries and forts encompassing the island. Antigua became one of the British Royal Navy's most important bases in the Caribbean.

an earthquake in 1843 followed by a hurricane in 1847 caused further hardship. Although most of the plantations were near to ruin, sugar was the only crop the islanders knew how to produce – and the only occupation open to them – it continued to be grown until well into the 20th century.

In 1860 Barbuda reverted to the British crown and was annexed by Antigua.

Late 19th century to the present

The Leeward Islands comprise of Anguilla, Antigua, Barbuda, Montserrat, St Kitts and Nevis, and in the late-19th century were governed by Britain as a single colony.

The islands remained part of the Leeward Islands Colony until this was broken up in 1956. In 1958 Antigua joined the West Indies Federation until it was dissolved in 1962. In February 1967, Antigua, led by former trade union leader Vere Cornwall Bird, became a State in Association with the United Kingdom with full control over its internal affairs, while Britain retained responsibility for external affairs and defending the islands.

The Independence movement continued to gain support throughout the 1970s, although its leader Prime Minister George Walter, was defeated in the 1976 elections by Vere Bird, who supported independence within a federation of

English Harbour from Shirley Heights

11

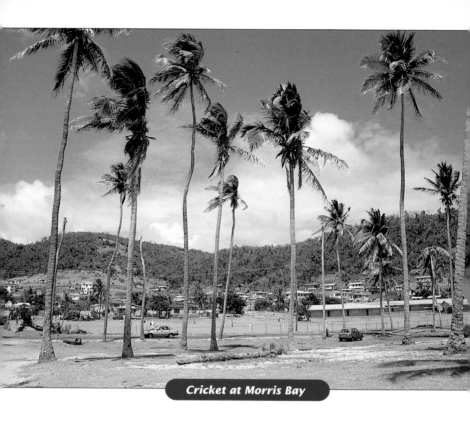

Cricket at Morris Bay

adjacent islands. In 1978 Bird changed his position and petitioned the British Government for immediate independence. Negotiations were complicated by the fact that Barbuda wanted to secede from Antigua. Eventually Barbuda agreed to unite with Antigua as an autonomous state and on 1 November 1981, the islands achieved their independence. Bird convincingly won the 1984 elections. Bird's son, Lester, was elected as leader of the Labour Party when his father stepped down in 1994, and is now Prime Minister. The three opposition parties joined forces as the United Progressive Party but in the 1999 General Election they won only five seats. The Antigua Labour Party took seven seats and the remaining seat was won by an independent representing Barbuda.

Antigua's reputation as a tourist destination really started to grow during the World War II when, under an agreement between the US and British, American forces were stationed on the island. There is still a defense base on the northeast coast of the island.

Climate

The near perfect year-round sub-tropical weather is one of the great attractions of Antigua and Barbuda. The sun nearly always shines and the two islands are among the driest in the Caribbean.

The average annual temperature is 79°F (26°C), with the average January and February temperatures – the 'coldest' months – about 77°F (25°C), and the average August temperature – the hottest month –

around 82°F (27.5°C). Summer temperatures rarely rise above 90°F (32°C), and there is usually a welcoming onshore breeze.

Annual rainfall is about 40 inches (102cm). November is the wettest month when about a quarter of the year's rain can fall, and showers are most frequent between September and December. It rains every month, but rarely for long and downpours may be sudden and heavy, but then the sun comes back out again. Humidity is highest in April and May and between August and December, with November having the highest humidity due to the high rainfall.

The People

The islands have a population of about 68,000, of which about ninety per cent are of African descent, the rest being European and North Americans. Most people (36,000) live in St John's, the capital of Antigua, while Codrington, the main settlement on Barbuda, has a population of about 1,000.

Hurricanes

Hurricane season lasts from June to November with September and October usually the busiest months for tropical storms.

Statistically only four hurricanes hit the islands every one hundred years, and 1995 was one of those years. That September, Hurricane Luis caused devastating damage on Barbuda with virtually every building affected, while on Antigua about two-thirds of the properties were damaged by the 100mph (161kmh) winds and high seas. The islanders started the clear-up operation and repairs immediately and most hotels quickly re-opened. In 1998, the islands were again hit, this time by Hurricane Georges but as before, damage was quickly repaired.

The Government has detailed hurricane contingency plans, including evacuation and storm shelters. If a hurricane threatens the islands, follow the advice given locally.

Culture and Festivals

Carnival is the major annual festival. It commemorates the abolition of slavery on 1 August 1834, and is now one huge, exuberant jump-up. It was first held on June 3, 1952 as a one day event as part of the Coronation celebrations for Queen Elizabeth II. Today, it takes place at the end of July and beginning of August and lasts for ten days with costume parades and lots and lots of partying and dancing. The Antigua Recreation Ground in St John's becomes a tented 'Carnival City' for the duration. In the calypso tents singers present their latest lyrics, always topical and often raunchy, and the Calypso King is crowned.

There are also musical offerings, food and drinks plus steel band competitions, the judging and crowning of the Carnival Queen, and a Caribbean Queens Competition. This is not a time for the faint-hearted, or those who like to take to their beds early, but it is a great festive occasion and one not to be missed, although you may well need a vacation afterwards to recover!

Antiguan music and dance features strong drum rhythms and is a lively mix of African and Caribbean. There are many excellent dance groups including the Obatala Performers and National Dance Group.

Antigua has also produced many fine artists, sculptors, potters and carvers such as Carl Henry, Sarah Fuller, Milton Henry, Nick Maley, Colin Martin, Nancy Nicholson, Priscilla Looby, Cadman Mathias, Yolanda Woodberry, Gilly Bobinet, Chinwe Osaze and Gilly Huntington Rainey.

Other main festivals

- **International Cricket Week** featuring the West Indies against visiting teams.
- **Tennis Week** is held in January and attracts top name seeds from the US and Europe.
- **Sailing Week** takes place at the end of April and beginning of May at English Harbour. It attracts entries from around the world for the racing, and provides an opportunity for near non-stop shore festivities.
- **Windsurfing Week** is staged in July in Dickenson Bay.

The Economy

Antigua's economy was originally based on agriculture, principally sugar cane, but tourism is now the major industry and income earner. Over 500,000 visitors arrive each year by air and sea.

There is some industry on Antigua producing clothing, paper goods, concrete blocks, beverages and some chemicals, and assembling electronic equipment. The soil on Barbuda was too poor to support sugar cane, and the land was used mostly for livestock farming although some cotton was grown. The island's economy, however, has long been based on fishing and subsistence farming, and the tourism industry is still in its infancy.

The view from Harmony Hall

The Government and Judiciary

Antigua and Barbuda is an independent state with a constitutional monarchy, with the British Queen Elizabeth II as the nominal head of state. She is represented on the island by the Governor-General. There is an elected seventeen-member House of Representatives and Senate, and executive power is in the hands of a Council of Ministers headed by the Prime Minister.

Flora and Fauna

The national flower is the Dagger Log (Agave Karatto) also called the Century Plant. The national fruit is the Antigua Black Pineapple.

The islands have a lush tropical vegetation despite the low rainfall in places, and the overall impression is of greenery and stunning flowers. There are wonderful displays of flowering flamboyants (the Royal Poinciana), bougainvillea, hibiscus and frangipani.

Along the roads you can spot giant ferns and massive stands of towering bamboo, sugar cane, bananas, coconut groves, hanging breadfruit, mango, nutmeg, cocoa and pawpaw, and the most stunning array of spectacular-looking flowering plants from giant African tulip trees festooned with scarlet blossom, to tiny orchids.

Many homes have charming gardens with flowers, vegetables and trees. The trees are important for shade and also because many provide fruit. Bougainvillea flowers everywhere and there are scores of varieties of hibiscus, frangipani and poinsettia. There are heliconia, also known as the lobster plant, bird of paradise flowers and anthurium everywhere. The flamboyant tree is also known as the tourist tree because it bursts into red bloom during the summer.

In areas of lower rainfall the vegetation consists of thorn, cactus, yucca, mesquite and woodland. These plants are drought resistant and can survive in a dormant state, sometimes for months, after losing all their leaves because of lack of moisture. Along the coast you can find swamps, mangroves and marsh woodlands.

Originally almost all of the island was covered by forest, but much of this was cleared to make way for the plantations. You can also spot mahogany and the white cedar as well as soursop, mango, coconut and breadfruit. Several species of orchid grow on the hillsides, many of them rare, and some so small that they can easily be overlooked. Close to the beach you can find red-barked turpentine trees and bearded figs.

Beach morning glory, with its array of pink flowers, is found on many beaches, and is important as its root system helps to prevent sand drift. The plant also produces nectar from glands in the base of its leaf stalks which attract ants, and it is thought this evolution has occurred so that the ants will discourage any leaf-nibbling predators. Other beach plants include seagrape and the manchineel, which should be treated with caution.

Carlisle Bay

A note of warning — the Manchineel

Found on many beaches the Manchineel has a number of effective defensive mechanisms which can prove very painful. Trees vary from a few feet to more than 30 feet in height, and have widely spreading, deep forked boughs with small, dark green leaves and yellow stems, and fruit like small, green apples. If you examine the leaves carefully without touching them, you will notice a small pin-head sized raised dot at the junction of leaf and leaf stalk. The apple-like fruit is very poisonous, and sap from the tree causes very painful blisters. It is so toxic, that early Caribs are said to have dipped their arrow heads in it before hunting trips. Sap is released if a leaf or branch is broken, and more so after rain. Avoid contact with the tree, don't sit under it, or on a fallen branch, and do not eat the fruit. If you do get sap on your skin, run into the sea and wash it off as quickly as possible.

Ocean life

The sea teems with brilliantly marked fish and often even more spectacular-looking coral and marine plants. Even if you just float upside down in the water with a face mask on you will be able to enjoy many of the beautiful underwater scenes, but the best way to see things is by scuba diving, snorkeling or taking a trip in a glass-bottomed boat.

There are scores of different corals, both hard and soft, that make up the reefs offshore. Only one, the fire coral poses a threat to swimmers and divers because if touched it causes a stinging skin rash.

Among the more spectacular corals are deadman's fingers, staghorn, brain coral and seafans, and there are also huge sea anemones and sponges.

Tropical fish species include the parrot fish, blue tang surgeon fish, tiny but aggressive damselfish, angelfish and wrasse.

Coastal swamps

A rich habitat for wildlife, tiny tree crabs and burrowing edible land crabs which scurry around in the mud trapped in the roots of mangrove trees just above water level. Herons, egrets, pelicans and often frigate birds roost in the higher branches, while the mangrove cuckoo shares the lower branches with belted kingfishers.

Plants

Gardens are often full of flowers in bloom year round, growing alongside exotic vegetables like yam, sweet potato, and dasheen.

Flowering plants include the flamboyant tree with its brilliant red flowers which burst into bloom in early summer, and long dark brown seed pods up to two feet

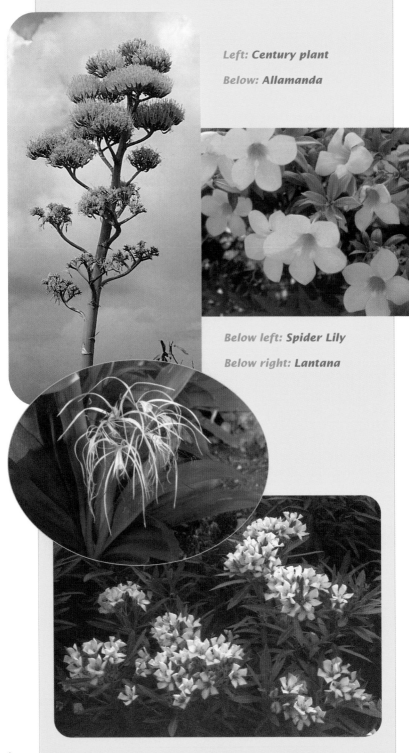

Left: *Century plant*

Below: *Allamanda*

Below left: *Spider Lily*

Below right: *Lantana*

long which can be used as rattles when the seeds have dried out inside. Bougainvillea grows everywhere and seems to be in bloom year round in a host of different shades. There are yellow and purple allamandas, poinsettia, hibiscus, anthurium and the ixora.

The leaves of the traveller's palm spread out like a giant open fan, the tree deriving its name from the belief that it pointed south to north, but it rarely does.

Along roadsides and hedgerows in the countryside, you can see the vine-like caralita, calabash with its gourd-like fruits, tamarind, and distinctive star-shaped leaves of the castor bean, whose seeds when crushed yield castor oil.

Areas of scrubland have their own flora or fauna, with plants bursting into flower following the first heavy rains after the dry season. Century plants, with their prickly, sword-like leaves, grow for up to twenty years before flowering. The yellow flower stalk grows at a tremendous rate for several days and can reach 20 feet (6m) high, but having bloomed once, the whole plant then dies. Other typical scrubland vegetation includes aloe, acacia, prickly pear and several species of cactus.

Animals

There are few large animals but in the dense woodlands on Barbuda there are fallow deer and a few wild pigs. The islands do, however, have a rich population of mini-reptiles, insects, butterflies, moths (some of them huge) and many species of bats. There are also scorpion and large centipedes.

There are several species of endangered turtle – leatherback, hawksbill and green – and, offshore, dolphins, whales and manatees can be seen. The manatee is the animal which early mariners thought was a mermaid – obviously after having been at sea for too long, or having drunk too much local rum.

Birds

The islands have a rich birdlife with 170 species recorded as residents or visiting migrants.

Species include the Zenaida dove (also known as the mountain dove), and ground dove, hummingbirds, ani, kingbird, grackle, thrushie, aggressive pearl-eyed thrasher, herons, egrets, mocking bird, bananaquit, grasssquit, smooth-billed ani, Caribbean martin and the hovering American kestrel.

The ani

A member of the cuckoo family, the ani is easily sighted by its dark plumage and parrot-like beak. It has a shrill squawking call, and strange and impractical nesting habits. The hen birds tend to lay their eggs in a communal nest. The first bird lays her eggs, the second lays her eggs on top and so on. The birds take it in turns to sit on the eggs but the eggs at the bottom of the pile do not get enough body heat for incubation, so they rarely hatch.

The gentle cooing of the zenaida dove is a familiar island noise.

Offshore you may see tropic-birds and the magnificent frigate bird. It has a long black 7-8 foot (2-2.5m) wing span, forked tail, and apparent effortless ability to glide on the winds. There are brown booby birds, named by sailors from the Spanish word for 'fool' because they were so easy to catch. Pelicans which look so un-gainly on land, yet are so acrobatic in the air, are common, as are laughing gulls and royal terns. Several species of sandpiper can usually be seen scurrying around at the water's edge.

Offshore islands have large bird populations, and on Great Bird Island you can see the red-billed tropic bird.

If you are really interested in bird watching, pack a small pair of binoculars. Mini-binoculars are ideal for island bird watching, because the light is normally so good that you will get a clear image despite the small object lens.

Fruits

As most of the plants, fruits, veg-etables and spices will be new to the first time visitor, the following brief descriptions are offered. A good place to learn more about the islands' fruits and vegetables, is to visit one of the farmers' markets.

Banana

Bananas are one of the Caribbean's most important exports, thus their nickname 'green gold' – and they grow everywhere. On Antigua and Barbuda, banana trees are usually called fig trees!

There are three types of banana plant; the banana that we normally buy in supermarkets originated in Malaya and were introduced into the Caribbean in the early 16th century by the Spanish. The large bananas, or plantains, originally came from southern India and the East Indies, and are largely used in cooking. They are often fried and served as an accompaniment to fish and meat. The third variety is the red banana, which is not grown commercially, and is quite rare.

Most banana plantations cover only a few acres (0.8 hectares) and are worked by the owner or tenant, although there are still some very large holdings. A banana produces a crop about every nine months, and each cluster of flowers grows into a hand of bananas. A bunch can contain up to twenty hands of bananas, with each hand having up to 20 individual fruit.

Although they grow tall, ban-anas are not trees but herbaceous plants which die back each year. Once the plant has produced fruit, a shoot from the ground is culti-vated to take its place, and the old plant dies.

Bananas need a lot of attention, and island farmers will tell you that there are not enough hours in a day to do everything that needs to be done. The crop needs feeding regu-larly, leaves need cutting back, and you will often see the fruit inside blue tinted plastic containers, which protect it from insect and bird attack, and speed up maturation.

Breadfruit

Breadfruit was introduced to the Caribbean by Captain Bligh in 1793. He brought 1,200 breadfruit

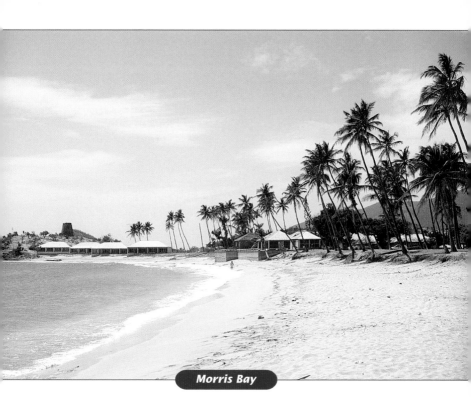

Morris Bay

Mutiny on the Bounty

It was Bligh's attempts to bring in young breadfruit trees that led to the mutiny on the *Bounty*. Bligh was given the command of the 215 ton *Bounty* in 1787 and was ordered to take the breadfruit trees from Tahiti to the West Indies where they were to be used to provide cheap food for the slaves.

The ship had collected its cargo and had reached Tonga when the crew under Fletcher Christian mutinied. The crew claimed that Bligh's regime was too tyrannical, and he and 18 members of the crew who stayed loyal to him, were cast adrift in an open boat. The cargo of breadfruit was dumped overboard. Bligh, in a remarkable feat of seamanship, navigated the boat for 3,600 miles (5800km) until making landfall on Timor in the East Indies.

Some authorities have claimed that it was the breadfruit tree cargo that sparked the mutiny, as each morning the hundreds of trees in their heavy containers had to be carried on deck, and then carried down into the hold at nightfall. It might have proved just too much for the already overworked crew.

saplings from Tahiti aboard the *Providence*, and these were first planted in Jamaica and St Vincent, and then quickly spread throughout the islands. The slaves did not like them at first, but the tree spread and can now be found almost everywhere.

Breadfruit is a cheap carbohydrate-rich food, although pretty tasteless when boiled. It is best eaten fried, baked or roasted over charcoal. It is often used as a potato substitute, and makes excellent crisps (chips) when finely sliced and deep fried. It has large dark, green leaves, and the large green fruits can weigh 10-12lbs (4.5-5.5kg). The falling fruits explode with a loud bang and splatter the pulpy contents over a large distance. It is said that no one goes hungry when the breadfruit is in season.

Calabash

Calabash trees are native to the Caribbean and have huge gourd like fruits which are very versatile when dried and cleaned. They can be used as water containers and bowls, bailers for boats, and as lanterns. Juice from the pulp is boiled into a concentrated syrup and used to treat coughs and colds, and the fruit is said to have many other medicinal uses.

Club Antigua

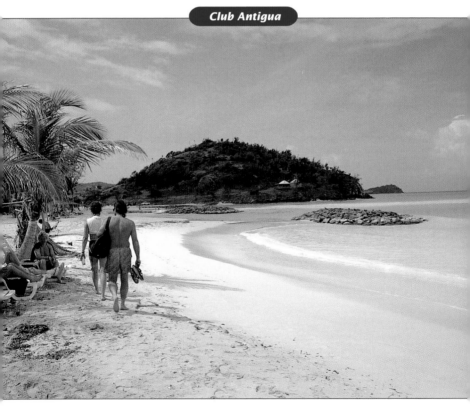

Cocoa

Cocoa is another important crop, and its Latin name *theobroma* means 'food of the gods'. A cocoa tree can produce several thousand flowers a year, but only a fraction of these will develop into seed bearing pods. It is the heavy orange pods that hang from the cocoa tree which contain the beans which contain the seeds that produce cocoa and chocolate. The beans, containing a sweet, white sap that protects the seeds, are split open and kept in trays to ferment. This process takes up to eight days and the seeds must be kept at a regular temperature to ensure the right taste and aroma develops. The seeds are then dried.

In the old days people used to walk barefoot over the beans to polish them to enhance their appearance. Today, the beans are crushed to extract cocoa butter, and the remaining powder is cocoa.

Real chocolate is produced by mixing cocoa powder, cocoa butter and sugar. You can sometimes buy cocoa balls in the markets which make a delicious drink. Each ball is the size of a large cherry. Simply dissolve the ball in a pan of boiling water, allow to simmer and then add sugar and milk or cream, for a rich chocolate drink. Each ball will make about four mugs of chocolate.

Coconut

Coconut palms are everywhere and should be treated with caution. Anyone who has heard the whoosh of a descending coconut and leapt to safety, knows how scary the sound is. Those who did not hear the whoosh, presumably did not live to tell the tale. Actually, very few people do get injured by falling coconuts and that is a near miracle in view of the tens of thousands of palms all over the island, but it is not a good idea to picnic in a coconut grove!

Coconut trees are incredibly hardy and able to grow in sand even when regularly washed by salty sea water. They can also survive long periods without rain. Their huge leaves, up to 20 feet (6m) long in mature trees, drop down during dry spells so a smaller surface area is exposed to the sun which reduces evaporation. Coconut palms can grow up to 80 feet (24m)tall, and produce up to 100 seeds a year. The seeds are the second largest in the plant kingdom, and these fall when ripe.

The coconut is the seed with its layer of coconut flesh surrounded by a hard shell. This shell is then surrounded by a layer of copra, a fibrous material, and this is covered by a large green husk. The seed and protective coverings can weigh 30lbs (13.5kg) and more.

The seed and casing are waterproof, drought proof and able to float, and this explains why coconut palms which originated in the Pacific and Indian Oceans, are now found throughout the Caribbean – the seeds literally floated across the seas.

The coconut palm is extremely versatile. The leaves can be used as thatch for roofing, or cut into strips and woven into mat and baskets, while the husks yield coir, which is resistant to salt water and ideal for ropes and brushes and brooms. Green coconuts contain a delicious

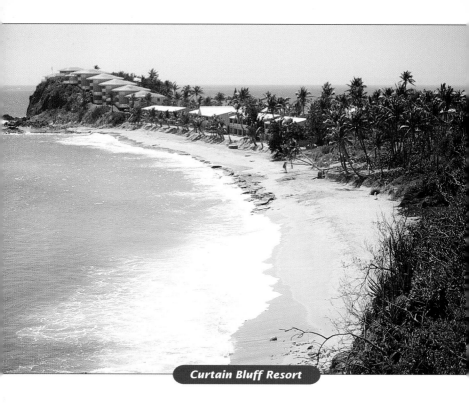

Curtain Bluff Resort

thirst-quenching 'milk', and the coconut 'meat' can be eaten raw, or baked in ovens for two days before being sent to processing plants where the oil is extracted. Coconut oil is used in cooking, soaps, synthetic rubber and even in hydraulic brake fluid.

As you drive around the island, you might see groups of men and women splitting the coconuts in half with machetes preparing them for the ovens. You might also see halved coconut shells spaced out on the corrugated tin roofs of some homes. These are being dried before being sold to the copra processing plants.

Dasheen

Dasheen is one of the crops known as 'ground provisions' in the Caribbean, the others being sweet potatoes, yams, eddo and tannia.

The last two are close relatives of dasheen, and all are members of the aroid family, some of the world's oldest cultivated crops.

Dasheen with its 'elephant ear' leaves, and eddo grow from a corm which when boiled thoroughly can be used like potato, and the young leaves of either are used to make calaloo (also spelled callaloo, kallaloo and several others ways). It is a spinach-like soup. Both dasheen and eddo are thought to have come from China or Japan but tannia is native to the Caribbean, and its roots can be boiled, baked or fried.

Guava

Guava is common throughout the West Indies, and the aromatic, sweet pink pulpy fruit is also sort after by birds who then distribute its seeds.

The fruit bearing shrub can be seen on roadsides and in gardens, and it is used to make a wide range of products from jelly to 'cheese', a paste made by mixing the fruit with sugar.

The fruit which ranges from a golf ball to a tennis ball in size, is a rich source of vitamin A and contains more vitamin C than citrus fruit. Because it contains many small seeds, it is best eaten as a jelly or as ice-cream, or drunk as juice. Guava juice is used as an ingredient in a number of tempting cocktails, but shouldn't be confused with the guavaberry, which also grows locally. The berries from this plant have been traditionally used by islanders to brew a special liqueur.

Mango

Mango can be delicious if somewhat messy to eat. It originally came from India and the East Indies, but is now grown throughout the Caribbean and found wherever there are people. Young mangoes can be stringy and unappealing, but ripe fruit from mature trees which grow up to 50 feet (15m) and more, are usually delicious, and can be eaten raw or cooked. The juice is a great reviver in the morning, and the fruit is often used to make jams and other preserves, and great ice-cream.

Royal Antiguan Hotel

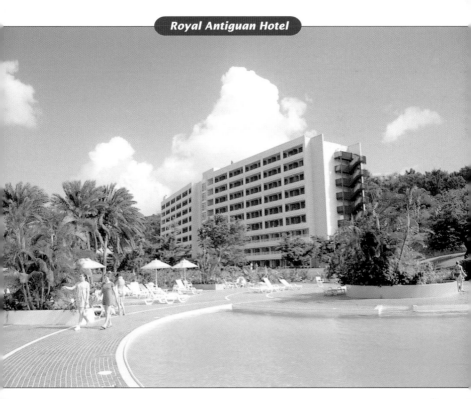

Nutmeg

Nutmeg trees are found on all the Caribbean islands. The tree thrives in hilly, wet areas and the fruit is the size of a small tomato. The outer husk, which splits open while still on the tree, is used to make the very popular nutmeg jelly. Inside, the seed is protected by a bright red casing which when dried and crushed produces the spice mace. Finally, the dark outer shell of the seed is broken open to reveal the nutmeg which is dried and then ground into a powder, or sold whole so that it can be grated to add taste to dishes.

Passion fruit

Passion fruit is not widely grown but it can usually be bought at the market. The pulpy fruit contains hundreds of tiny seeds, and many people prefer to press the fruit and drink the juice. It is also commonly used in fruit salads, sherbets and ice-creams.

Pawpaw

Pawpaw or papaya trees are also found throughout the islands and are commonly grown in gardens. The trees are prolific fruit producers but grow so quickly that the fruit soon becomes difficult to gather. The large, juicy melon-like fruits are eaten fresh, pulped for juice or used locally to make jams, preserves and ice cream. They are rich sources of vitamin A and C.

The leaves and fruit contain an enzyme which softens meat, and tough joints cooked wrapped in pawpaw leaves or covered in slices of fruit, usually taste like much more expensive cuts. The same enzyme, papain, is also used in chewing gum, cosmetics, the tanning industry and, somehow, in making wool shrink resistant. A tea made from unripe fruit is said to be good for lowering high blood pressure. Ripe papaya slices and lime make a delicious, healthy breakfast.

Pigeon peas

Pigeon peas are widely cultivated and can be found in many back gardens. The plants are very hardy and drought resistant, and produce prolific yields of peas which can be eaten fresh or dried and used in soups and stews.

Pineapples

Pineapples were certainly grown in the Caribbean by the time Columbus arrived, and were probably brought from South America by the Amerindians. The fruit is slightly smaller than the Pacific pineapple, but taste more intense, especially if you have not tried a really fresh pineapple before.

Antigua's smaller 'black' pineapples are particularly succulent, and a prized export. Most fruit for export is picked before it is ripe so that it arrives many days later in reasonable condition. Really ripe fruit straight from the tree has an intense aroma, bursts with juice, and has almost no core, as this only develops as it ages.

Plantain

Plantain are another import from the East Indies and not to be confused with their cousins, the smaller yellow banana. Plantain are bigger, more versatile and a staple part of the Caribbean diet,

The Tamarind

Originally from India, the tamarind is now a common sight throughout the Caribbean. The trees can grow very tall and bushy, and are long living, with dangling bulbous pods, that contain the rather tart fruit. The edible part is the pulp that surrounds the seeds, and it makes a delicious drink, and is also often added to curries and seasonings. It is also one of the special ingredients in Lea and Perrins Worcestershire sauce which makes it so distinctive. It is even said that the pulp can be used to bring back the shine to tarnished brass and copper.

Quite often the area around the base of tamarind is devoid of other vegetation, because the tree's roots give out a toxic chemical which kills off other plants.

and must always be cooked before eating.

One way of identifying bananas and plantain on the tree, is that banana fingers on the hand generally point up, while plantain fingers normally point down, or so I am assured.

Other fruits

Soursop is a member of the same family as the sugar apple, and its spiny, pulpy fruits can be seen growing in hedgerows and gardens. They are eaten fresh, although they have lots of little black seeds, or used for preserves, drinks and ice cream.

Sugar apple is a member of the annona fruit family, and grows wild and in gardens throughout the islands. It is also called the custard apple and sweetsop, because it is a lot sweeter than the soursop. The small, soft sugar apple can be peeled off in strips when ripe, and is like eating thick apple sauce. They are eaten fresh or used to make sherbet or drinks.

Sugar Cane is still grown in gardens but not commercially. All of the cane grown to produce molasses for the rum industry is imported. The canes can grow up to 12 feet (3.5m) tall and after cutting, the canes have to be crushed to extract the sugary juice. After extraction, the juice is boiled until the sugar crystals are formed. The mixture remaining is molasses and this is used to produce rum.

Food

Antigua offers a huge choice when it comes to eating out, from excellent traditional island fare to the finest international cuisine at the best tourist hotels.

Dining out offers the chance to experiment with all sorts of unusual spices, vegetables and fruits, with Creole and island dishes, and, of course, rum punches and other exotic cocktails.

Eating out is very relaxed and most restaurants do not have a strict dress code, although most people like to wear something a little smarter at dinner after a day on the beach or out sightseeing. Many hotels have a tendency to offer buffet dinners or barbecues, but even these can be interesting and tasty affairs.

Breakfast

Breakfast can be one of the most exciting meals of the day for a visitor. There is a huge range of fruit juices to choose from. Try a glass of water melon juice, followed by a fresh grapefruit, or slices of chilled pawpaw or mango. Most hotels offer fruit plates containing a wide choice, so you should be able to taste your way through them all during your stay.

The island's fruits also make great jams and preserves, and you can follow the fruit with piping hot toast spread with citrus marmalade or guava jam. Most tourist hotels also offer traditional American breakfasts for those who can't do without them.

During the summer there are fruits such as the kenip, plumrose, sugar apple and yellow plum. Green bananas and plantains are usually eaten raw, or boiled or steamed in the skin, then cut into slices and served very hot. They also make excellent chips when fried.

Jolly Castle Marina

Starters

Starters include a huge choice of fruit juices from orange and grapefruit to the more unusual ones like soursop and tamarind. You can also drink green coconut 'milk'.

Traditional Caribbean starters also include dishes such as Christophène and coconut soup, and Callaloo soup made from the young leaves of dasheen or eddo, a spinach-like vegetable. The soup is made throughout the Caribbean and ochros, smoked meat and sometimes crab are added, as well as lots of herbs and spices. Chicken nuggets and marinated green bananas are also popular.

Fish and clam chowders are also popular starters. Try heart of palm, excellent fresh shrimps or scallops, smoked kingfish wrapped in crêpes, or crab backs – succulent land crab meat sautéd with breadcrumbs and seasoning, and served re-stuffed in the shell. It is much sweeter than the meat of sea crabs.

Fish & seafood

The fish is generally excellent, and don't be alarmed if you see dolphin on the menu. It is not the protected species made famous by 'Flipper', but a solid, close-textured flat faced fish called the dorado, which is delicious. Saltfish often appears on the menu. Salting was the most common form of preserving food, and allowed surplus catches to be kept safely until times of food shortage, or for when the seas were too rough for the fishing boats to go out.

Also available are snapper, grouper, kingfish, redfish, jacks, balaouy, tuna, flying fish, lobster, swordfish, baby squid and mussels. There are delicious river crayfish and the larger saltwater variety, mussels and oyster.

Try seafood jambalaya – chunks of lobster, shrimps and ham served on a bed of braised seasoned rice; shrimp Creole – fresh shrimp sautéd in garlic butter and parsley and served with tomatoes; or fish Creole – fresh fish steaks cooked in a spicy onion, garlic and tomato sauce and served with rice and fried plantain.

Island 'fast food'

Island fast food includes patties, which are pastry cases stuffed with meats or saltfish, fritters and roti, which was brought to the islands by East Indian indentured workers in the nineteenth century. It consists of a thin dough wrapped around a hot spicy curry mixture containing beef, chicken, vegetables or fish. The chicken roti often contains small bones which some people like to chew on, so be warned.

For vegetarians there are excellent salads, stuffed breadfruit, callaloo bake, stuffed squash and pawpaw, and baked sweet potato and yam casserole.

Desserts

For dessert, try fresh fruit salad, with added cherry juice, and some-times a little rum, a year-round popular dessert. There is a wide variety of fruit sherbets using tropical fruits such as soursop and tamarind.

Or try one of the exotic tasting ice-creams. There are also banana fritters and banana flambé, coconut cheesecake, and green papaya or guava shells simmered in heavy syrup.

Buffet

On the buffet table you will often see a dish called pepper pot. This is usually a hot, spicy meat and vegetable stew to which may be added small flour dumplings and shrimps. Pepperpot and fungee is the national dish. Fungee is a sort of dumpling made from cornmeal and okra.

Another note of warning

On most tables you will find a bottle of pepper sauce. It usually contains a blend of several types of hot pepper, spices and vinegar, and should be treated cautiously. Try a little first, before splashing it all over your food, as these sauces range from hot to unbearable.

If you want to make your own hot pepper sauce, take four ripe hot peppers, one teaspoon each of oil, ketchup and vinegar, and a pinch of salt, blend together into a liquid and bottle.

There are also wonderful breads, and you should try them if you get the chance. There are banana and pumpkin breads, and delicious cakes such as coconut loaf cake, guava jelly cookies and rum cake.

Drinks

Rum is the Caribbean drink. There are almost as many rums in the West Indies as there are malt whiskies in Scotland, and there is an amazing variety of strength, hue and quality. The first West Indian rum was produced in the Danish Virgin Islands in the 1660s and by the end of the century, there were thousands of distilleries throughout the Caribbean. Rum rapidly became an important commodity and figured prominently in the infamous Triangle Trade in which slaves from Africa were sold in Europe for rum in the West Indies which was sold to raise money to buy more slaves.

Rum has such fortifying powers that General George Washington insisted every soldier be given a daily tot, and a daily ration also became a tradition in the British Royal Navy, one that lasted from the 18th century until 1970.

Columbus is credited with planting the first sugar cane in the Caribbean, on Hispaniola, during his third voyage, and the Spanish called the drink produced from it aguardiente de cane, although it was officially named as saccharum, from the Latin name for sugar cane. It was English sailors who abbreviated this name to rum. It is sometimes suggested that the word rum comes from an abbreviation of the word 'rumbullion'. While the origin of this word is unknown there is a record of it in 1672, and it was later used to describe a drunken brawl.

Rum can be produced in two ways. It can be distilled directly from the fermented juice of crushed sugar cane, or made from molasses which is produced after the sugar, extracted from the cane by crushing, has been boiled until crystals form. Dark rums need keeping for many years in oak barrels, sometimes for up to 15. White rum is light bodied and require less time in the barrel.

The excellent English Harbour Rum is one of those distilled, blended and bottled on the island by The Antigua Distillery Ltd. They also produce the popular Cavalier range of rums. Rum shops are a popular feature of island life and there are usually one or two in each village. Like the English pub, they are focal points where people gather to have a drink, exchange gossip and play dominoes or warri. They are usually noisy places but don't confuse the raised voices as anger – people just have to shout in order to be heard. Rum shops also serve good, cheap local food

– usually chicken and fresh fish.

Island beer is good, Wadadli being the most popular brew of the Antigua Brewery. The brewery began production in 1993, and the lager beer is named after the original Arawak word for the island. It is light and refreshing, and available both on tap and bottled.

Most tourist hotels and bars offer a wide range of cocktails both alcoholic (usually very strong) and non-alcoholic. Tap water is safe to drink and mineral and bottled water is widely available, as are soft drinks.

Note: While many of the main tourist hotel restaurants offer excellent service, time does not have the same urgency as it does back home, and why should it after all, as you are on holiday. Relax, enjoy a drink, the company and the surroundings and don't worry if things take longer – the wait is generally worth it!

Mix your own!

Painkiller

The Painkiller is a rum cocktail containing orange and pineapple juice, cream of coconut and a sprinkling of nutmeg.

Plantation Rum Punch

There are scores of different rum cocktails, and one of the most popular is the traditional Caribbean Plantation Rum Punch.
To make, thoroughly mix 3 ounces of rum, with one ounce of lime juice and one teaspoon of honey, then pour over crushed ice, and for a little zest, add a pinch of freshly grated nutmeg.

Planter's Punch

Combine 2 ounces each of pineapple juice, rum, cream of coconut and half an ounce of lime in a blender for one minute. Pour into a chilled glass, add a sprinkle of grated coconut and garnish with a slice of cherry and a slice of orange.

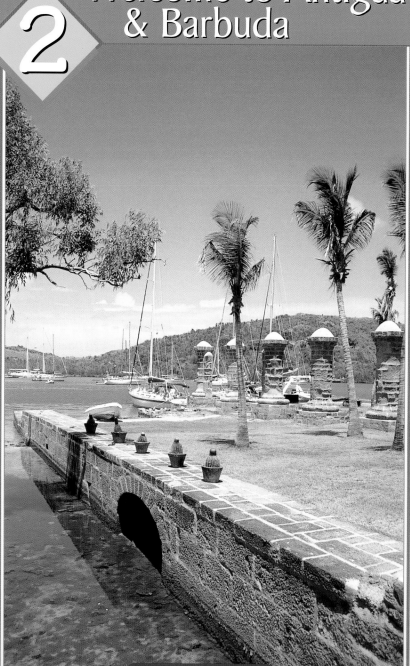

Nelson's Dockyard

Getting around Antigua

By road

Antigua has almost 625 miles (1000km) of roads and nearly all of the island is accessible, although conditions vary considerably. Many roads are not signposted at all even in towns, and some are unpaved. Great care needs to be taken off the main roads because of pot holes and other surface damage and erosion. After heavy rains debris can also be washed on to the roads.

You can explore by rental car or taxi, and bicycles, which can be rented, also offer an excellent way to get around.

Taxis

Taxis are available at the VC Bird International Airport, most hotels, and in St John's. There are fixed taxi fares between the airport and most island destinations, and you can negotiate your own deals for excursions and tours. Fixed fares are posted at the airport. Always make sure when negotiating a taxi fare that you know which currency you dealing in – US$ or EC$: it could save an unpleasant situation later.

By bus

There are some bus routes operating to and from St John's, but they tend to run into St John's in the morning, and out of the capital late in the afternoon taking workers home. There are almost no services during the evening or on Sunday. The most regular service, and the most useful, is between St John's and English Harbour. Buses leave the West Bus Station, which is on the waterfront off Valley Road and conveniently across from the Market, for the southern part of the island; and from the East Bus Station across from Independence Avenue by its junction with Factory Road, for the north and eastern parts. Exploring by bus is a great way of getting around and meeting the islanders, and it is also cheap.

By air

LIAT, the regional airline, flies between Antigua and twenty-five Caribbean islands, and schedules are timed so that day trips are possible. Carib Aviation, a charter company based at VC Bird International Airport, also offers day tours in addition to its regular charter flights.

By sea

There are several boats offering trips to Barbuda, and yachts are available for charter, either crewed or bare-board for exploring off-shore islands and secluded bays. You can also charter a boat to visit the bird island of Redonda.

ANTIGUA

N
W · · · E
S

Boon Point

Gambles Golf Course

Beggars Poin

Rex Halcyon Cove Beach Resort

Dickenson Bay

Sandals Antigua Resort

Cedar Grove

Coolidge

Runaway Bay

New Winthorpes

Antigua International Airport

Sh Po

Barnes Hill

Fort James

Fort James Bay

ST JOHN'S

Deep Bay

Galley Bay

Yepton Beach Resort

St John's Harbour

St Johnston Village

Fitches Creek

Five Islands Village

Hawksbill Resort/Bay

Potters Village

SAINT GEORGE

Five Islands Harbour

Pearns Point

Mosquito Bay

Jennings

SAINT JOHN

Freemah

Lignumvitae Bay

Bolans

Jolly Beach

Jolly Harbour

A Sain

Ffryes Point

SAINT MARY

Swetes

John Hughes

Liberta

Darkwood Beach

★ Boggy Peak

Crab Hill

Johnsons Point

Urlings

Johnsons Bay

Cades Bay

Old Road

Falm

Morris Bay

Carlisle Bay

Rendezvous Bay

Doigs Beach

CARIBBEAN SEA

Long
Island

*iden
and*

*Barnacle
Point*

N o r t h

S o u n d

Guiana
Island

*rnham
arbour*

Crabs Peninsula

ATLANTIC
OCEAN

Guiana Bay

ham

*Mercers Creek
Bay*

*Long
Bay*

Indian Town Point

SAINT PETER

Seatons

★ Devil's Bridge

Pares

Willikies

Betty's ★
Hope Mill

Glanvilles

*Nonsuch
Bay*

*Green
Island*

works Dam Reservoir

★
Harmony
Hall

Newfield

SAINT PHILIP

Freetown

*Exchange Bay
Half Moon Bay*

Bethesda

*Willoughby
Bay*

Christian Hill

Cobbs
nk's Cross
ll

*ath
ur*

English
Harbour
Town

Dow
Interpreta-
tion
Centre

**St James's
Club**

■

*Mamora
Reef*

Mamora Bay

*n's
ard* ★

★
★ Shirley
Heights

*English
Harbour*

Cape Shirley

0		1		2 miles

0		2km	

• ST JOHN'S •

The island capital is one of the oldest trading ports in the Caribbean with a 300-year history. It still has many historic buildings although most of these date from the last 150 years. Earlier buildings, constructed of wood, were destroyed over the centuries either by fire, or by hurricanes and earthquakes.

Redcliffe Quay, St John's

Walking tour

The capital is easy to get around by foot as it is laid out in a grid, a legacy of the many natural disasters which allowed the town planners to rebuild from scratch. Driving, however, can be a problem until you get used to the one-way system. If you remember that streets run parallel with each other and you can't turn into the one you want,

simply follow the one way system round the block to gain access.

While some modern concrete structures have gone up, the town retains its charm through its fine old wooden and stone buildings, many brightly painted in pastels, and their overhanging balconies and shutters. Traditionally, town homes would have a stone-built ground floor with a wooden story above.

There are the up-market shopping

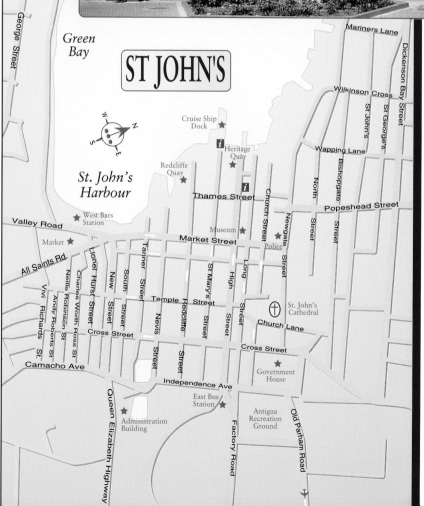

Heritage Quay, St John's

ST JOHN'S

Green Bay

St. John's Harbour

Cruise Ship Dock

Heritage Quay

Redcliffe Quay

Thames Street

West Bars Station

Valley Road

Market

All Saints Rd.

Market Street

Museum

Police

Church Street

Newgate Street

North Street

Popeshead Street

Mariners Lane

Dickenson Bay Street

Wilkinson Cross

St John's Street

St George's Street

Wapping Lane

Bishopgate Street

Lionel Hurst Street

Tanner Street

New Street

South Street

Charles Worth Ross St

Neille Worth Ross St

Andy Roberts St

Vivi Richards St.

Temple Street

Nevis Street

Redcliffe Street

St Mary's Street

High Street

Long Street

Church Lane

St. John's Cathedral

Cross Street

Cross Street

Camacho Ave

Independence Ave

Government House

East Bus Station

Queen Elizabeth Highway

Administration Building

Factory Road

Antigua Recreation Ground

Old Parham Road

complexes at Heritage Quay and Redcliffe Quay, but also many other types of stores to be visited on the streets in from the waterfront. To the south is the old market where island fruits and vegetables are sold, and along the waterfront on the outskirts of town fishing boats are hauled up on the beach, while the fishermen repair their nets and sell their catches. The Woods Centre is a new shopping area on the Friar's Hill Road on the outskirts of St John's, comprising super-markets, stores, banks, pharmacy, beauty salon, restaurants and a food court. It is open daily to 10pm.

Most of the main sights, how-ever, are in St John's, close to the waterfront, and contained within a few blocks.

The **Tourist Information Office** is on the corner of Thames and High Streets, where you can find out what is going on and if there are any special events taking place. The **Post Office** is a short step away towards the waterfront, and the **Cenotaph**, which commemorates those Antiguans who died during the two World Wars, stands at the top of the High Street. At the other end is the **Westerby Memo-rial**, erected in 1892 in memory of Bishop George Westerby and his Moravian missionaries. Between the Post Office and the Old Administration Building is the VC Bird Monument, in memory of Dr Vere Cornwall Bird, the first Premier. It was unveiled in 1987.

Antigua is one of the most popular cruise ship destinations in the Caribbean and most ships arrive at the modern **Cruise Ship Dock**. The ships are then able to disgorge their passen-gers straight into the heart of the town through Heritage Quay, a relatively new tourist development close to the Cruise Ship Dock with information desk, the Heritage Hotel, more than 40 duty free shops, restaurant and casino.

Kings Casino is the largest casino on the island with nightly gam-bling and entertainment. The casino features The King Machine, the world's largest slot machine, and a sports lounge with four televisions and a 10 foot (3m) screen. It is open Monday to Saturday from 10am to 4am, and on Sunday from 6pm to 4am ☎ 462-1727.

The quay at St John's is a popular port of call

· Shopping ·

Heritage Quay offers world class shopping at bargain prices, with top name stores selling a wide range of goods from clothing, to leather goods and arts and crafts. It is the only duty-free shopping area on Antigua. Shops include:

Aqua Sports – snorkeling and fishing gear.

Athlete's Foot – top name trainers and athletic shoes.

Benjies Photo Centre – cameras, film, quick processing, accessories, picture frames, sunglasses.

Caribbean Gems – gold and fine jewels, tennis bracelets and loose diamonds, and watches.

Caribbean Trading Post – hand-painted bags, T-shirts, island arts and crafts.

Colombian Emeralds International – the world's largest emerald retailer, also sells other stones and quality watches.

Gucci – watches, perfumes, gift items and leather goods.

Heritage Sports – sports clothing and equipment and swimwear.

Intrigue Boutique – Liz Clairborne Collection plus silver rings, necklaces, etc.

Island Arts – Caribbean art and hand-crafted items.

J. C. M. Jewellery – custom-made items and fine gifts.

La Casa del Habano – top quality cigars, pipes and tobaccos.

La Parfumerie – perfumes and cosmetics.

The Linen Shop – hand-embroidered linen and cotton goods and gifts.

Little Switzerland – rings, necklaces, etc, watches, crystal, chinaware, pens and fragrances.

Quin Farara's Liquor Stores – fine wines, spirits and tobacco.

West Indies Ice Company – a factory jewel and ring outlet designed to look like an old waterfront ice house, with savings of at least fifty per cent.

Redcliffe Quay is a short walk to the south along the Harbour. It is a delightful historic waterfront area with well restored nineteenth century buildings and warehouses now the home of shops and restaurants. The Quay has a wide range of shops selling everything from clothing to videos and toys. Of special interest are:

Base – offers superb contemporary designer clothing, created and produced on the premises.

Bona –gifts, antiques in china and silver, and modern china and glass.

Dalila – handicrafts and tropical clothing.

The Goldsmitty – hand-made jewels, designed and crafted by owner Hans Smit, plus other pieces.

Island Woman – Carribean and Balinese fashions.

Jacaranda –fine collection of island perfumes, cosmetics, herbs, spices, batik clothing and island arts and crafts.

Seahorse Studios – works by local and Caribbean artists, and island jewels and crafts.

Further south is the **West Bus Station** where you can catch buses to the south of the island and English Harbour. **The Market** is at the junction of Valley Road and All Saints Road, and always worth a visit not just for the sheer vibrancy, but also for the chance to haggle over delicious fruits. On sale is a huge array of island produce from fruits and vegetables to exotics herbs and spices. At the end of All Saint Road is the Industrial School for the Blind, a workshop where you can see the skilled weavers at work and buy their products ☎ 462-0663. From the Market, head back into town, then turn right on to New Street and cross over to the Queen Elizabeth Highway. On your right is the **Holy Family Cathedral** and on your left, the **Government Administration Buildings.**

Return to Independence Avenue and turn right with **Country Pond** on your left. Further along is the

St John's Cathedral

Built originally in wood between 1681 and 1683, the Cathedral was rebuilt in stone between 1742 and 1745 but destroyed by a massive earthquake almost a century later in 1843. The cornerstone of the present building was laid in 1845. The Cathedral, having been elevated to that status in 1842, was consecrated in 1848.

The stone cathedral with its twin towers has an unusual interior – it is encased in wood, designed to protect it from both earthquake and hurricane and has obviously been successful, as it has withstood both many times since.

The two statues at the south entrance of the Cathedral are of St John the Baptist and St John the Apostle. They were sculpted in the eighteenth century and were bound for Dominica, then controlled by the French, aboard a ship that was captured by a British Royal Navy vessel. The 'liberated' statues were brought to Antigua and later presented to the Cathedral.

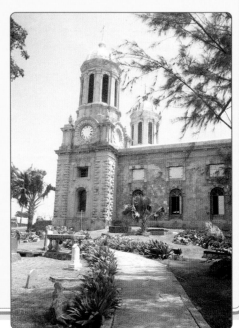

East Bus Station across the junction on your right, then you pass the **Antigua Recreation Ground** on your left, and **Government House** on your left. Government House was originally two buildings but they were joined and considerably extended. It is noted for its impressive two-floor colonnade and impressive early 19th century interior ☎ 462-0003.

Return to Long Street and turn left and then left again into Church Street and the Anglican St John's Cathedral. Continue along Church Street and then turn right into Market Street past the **police station** on the corner. This used to be a munitions store and nearby is the old guardhouse and the island's first jail.

Cross over Church Street and visit **The National Museum of Antigua and Barbuda,** on the corner of Market and Long Streets. It is in the **Old Court House**, the oldest building still in use in the capital. Designed by Peter Harrison, it was started in 1747 and opened three years later, but has had to be rebuilt a number of times because of natural disaster damage. The building was constructed of yellow free stone quarried on Long Island, Guana Island and Pelican Island. The court was on the ground floor and the Council and Assembly met upstairs. Although the building and exhibits are historic, the museum's approach to learning is not. The museum was opened in 1985 and is now a popular educational and research facility, with a fine library and National Archives. The museum traces the island's history from pre-Columbian times to Independence, and many of the exhibits encourage a 'hands-on' approach with 'please touch' signs aimed especially at children. There are displays about the island's geology, a life-size Arawak hut, a working 1829 steam engine once used to cut sugar cane, and a model of a sugar plantation. A container full of pieces of broken seventeenth century china invites you to try to put all the pieces together. The museum has a calendar of regularly changing special exhibits and is also the home of the Historical and Archaeological Society and the Environmental Awareness Group. There is a small gift shop which is open Monday to Friday from 8.30am to 4pm, and on Saturday from 10am to 2pm ☎ 462-4939. Admission is free but donations are appreciated.

The Botanic Gardens

The Gardens were first opened in 1888 and moved to their present site, close to the Parliament Building, five years later. The site originally covered 8 acres (3 hectares) and was used by the Government for agricultural research into plants that could be grown commercially. The gardens closed in 1950 and quickly became overgrown but at the end of the 1980s a committee was set up to restore them, and now you can enjoy their work. The garden has a wide range of plants found on the island and has a rich bird and animal life too.

• ISLAND TOURS •

While nearly all of Antigua can be reached by car, either on main or secondary roads, it is often necessary to retrace your route a small distance in order to continue with your tour. There are lots of side roads to explore and with 365 beaches around the island, you can usually get one all to yourself. Don't drive too fast because most road junctions are not marked. If you over-shoot your road drive on and turn round when safe to do so. If you get lost, simply ask an islander.

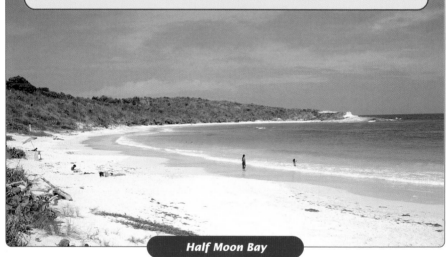

Half Moon Bay

TOUR 1 — The South

Head south out of St John's and then follow the road which runs south of the Harbour to **Five Islands**, a peninsula with a number of hotels and fine beaches. It is not easy to find the road as there are few signposts, but you turn by the King George Playing Fields. The road runs through the shanty town suburbs of St John's. Once you are out in open country the first main turning on your right heads for the sea and on top of Goat Hill are the remains of **Fort Barrington** built, like Fort James, to protect St John's Harbour as well as Deep Bay to the east. The best way to reach the fort is from the track which runs up the hill from the northern end of Deep Bay.

Fort Barrington

This fort has seen more action than any other on the island. It is not known when the original structure was built, but in 1652 Prince Rupert and Royalist forces captured the fort and used the cannon to sink one ship anchored in Deep Bay and force the surrender of a second. In 1666 the French attacked the island and captured the fort, but were forced to return it to the English in 1667.

The present fort dates from 1779-80 and was named in memory of Admiral Barrington who, a year earlier, had defeated the French at the Battle of Cul de Sac which restored St Lucia back to the British. There is a plaque in memory of William Burt, who was Governor when the fort was built. He is recorded as 'Emperor and Governor of the Leeward Islands'. The fort served as a signal station until 1960.

Deep Bay is a popular beach and dive site. The star attraction is the wreck of the freighter *Andes*, which sank in the mouth of the bay in 1907, and lies in just 20 feet (6m) of water.

Retrace your route back to the main road then drive south through Golden Grove and Ebeneezer. Cedar Hall and Green Castle Hill are on your left as you drive on to Jennings. There are a number of megaliths on top of the 565-foot (172m) high Greencastle Hill, which is an old volcano. There are excellent panoramic views from the summit. Many side trips can be taken along this route, such as the short detour west to Mosquito Cove and Pearns Point.

There are many beautiful beaches along this south-western stretch of coastline, and while they are not all easy to reach, the effort is always worthwhile.

The road then cuts closer to the coast at **Lignumvitae Bay**, named after the hardwood that used to grow just inland from there. Today the bay has hotels, restaurants and shops and is a popular tourist beach.

Jolly Harbour Marina and Shopping Centre, at Lignumvitae Bay, offers the opportunity for souvenir shopping with restaurants and bars to sustain you before, during and after. It is the home of the Jolly Harbour Yacht Club and the Carib Cup Regatta. Shops offer a wide range of goods from beach wear to arts and crafts, and curios from around the world to the latest electrical gadgetry. There are berths for 150 yachts, also ships' chandlers, a tackle and bait shop and boat repair yards. Jacaranda offers island cosmetics, herbs, spices, batik wear and local arts and crafts; Merry's Gift Shop has Caribbean arts and crafts; and the Seahorse Studios offers a variety of art originals, crafts, T-shirts, pottery and batik.

Excavations at Jolly Harbour have found a settlement dating back to 1775.

Follow the coast road round through Crab Hill to **Johnsons**

• Island Forts •

For much of its early life Antigua was surrounded by hostile European powers and the island was attacked by French, Spanish and Dutch pirates. When war broke out between the European powers it usually resulted in conflict in the Caribbean as their respective navies fought it out in the offshore waters. Because of its strategic importance, a ring of forts was built in the seventeenth and eighteenth centuries to protect the island, its busy quays and the hugely profitable sugar crop.

More than forty forts were built, some of them huge constructions covering many acres and taking a decade or more to finish. In an official report in 1734 Governor William Matthews listed twenty-seven manned forts around the island with a total of one hundred and thirty-three cannon. The largest was Fort George with thirty-three cannon, followed by Fort James with sixteen, Fort Berkeley with twelve, and Fort Charles with ten. Many of the forts were little more than small gun emplacements with just one or two cannon, and few ever had to fire their cannon in action.

Following Britain's defeat of France and the end of the Napoleonic Wars, the French no longer posed a threat in the Caribbean and the forts were gradually run down. Luckily, some survive, albeit as ruins, and can still be visited. Some of the cannon remain in place, but most of the weaponry has long been removed, and either sold as scrap or incorporated into the island landscape as traffic bollards.

Main forts	*Lesser forts*	
Codrington	Dickenson Bay	Hamilton Point
Dow's Hill	Falmouth	Hawk's Nest
Fort Barrington	Fort Byam	High Point
Fort Berkely	Fort Charles	Mercer's Creek
Fort James	Fort Isaac	Old Road Fort
Fort George	Fort William	
Fort Shirley		

If you want to learn more about the forts, visit the National Museum in St John's.

Point on the south-west corner of the island, where there are the remains of an eighteenth century fort. Inland are the Shekerley Mountains, the highest hills on the island, with **Boggy Peak** the highest point. A short way beyond Urlings is Brooks Old Mill, just inland from Cades Bay, and the road then runs on to Old Road. There is a small road inland from Cades Bay which allows access to Boggy Peak, and the climb to the summit is worth it for the stunning views. On a day free from heat-haze you can usually see Guadeloupe to the south and St Kitts to the north.

Old Road was the site of the first English settlement on Antigua and the fort was built to protect Carlisle Bay. Many place names include the word 'road' which is an old nautical term for a safe anchorage.

Fig Tree Drive

This is an ancient road that runs from Old Road, at the head of Carlisle Bay, inland round Signal Hill and Sugar Loaf Hill, before turning south at Swetes for **Liberta**. It winds its way inland through the steep sided, densely wooded hills covered in lush tropical vegetation. This was one of the island's main sugar cane growing areas as evidenced by the many old sugar mills along the way.

There are also several pretty churches, an indicator of how large the area's population must have been in the late eighteenth and nineteenth centuries. The most spectacular of these churches is the pink **Tyrell's Roman Catholic Church** on the main road just north of the Swetes junction. The drive is very pretty although the road is a bit rough in places and it gets its name from the banana trees along the way, known locally as fig trees. You can also see guava, mango and coconut.

Tyrell's Roman Catholic Church

Falmouth Harbour

Falmouth Harbour has provided safe anchorage for more than 400 years, and Falmouth is one of the island's oldest settlements. Work on the fortifications to defend the Harbour to the south started in 1669. The fort was huge covering an area of 7 acres (3hectares) and took sixteen years to complete.

The tall perimeter walls survive largely intact. Inside are the ruins of many of the old military buildings and structures, including cisterns for storing precious water supplies, and the magazines for holding the powder for the battery of thirty-two cannon. Nowadays the Harbour is as busy as ever catering to charter vessels and yachts from around the world.

Climbing up the hill you come to the village of John Hughes where you can park and take the nature trail which leads through the Wallings Forest of deciduous trees to a Victorian dam and reservoir about half a mile (0.8km) away. The dam took three years to build and was completed in 1893.

To the south-east of Liberta, and to the east of the road, is Monk's Hill on top of which are the ruins of **Fort George**. You can reach the fort by taking the side road to the village of Table Hill Gordon. From there it is about a mile (1.6km) to the fort. If you do not have a four-wheel-drive vehicle you will have to walk there and back. The hill is named after General Monk, Duke of Albemarle, and although known as Monk's Hill fort, its original name was Great George Fort, after the English patron saint.

The road then runs south into **Falmouth**, one of the coastal

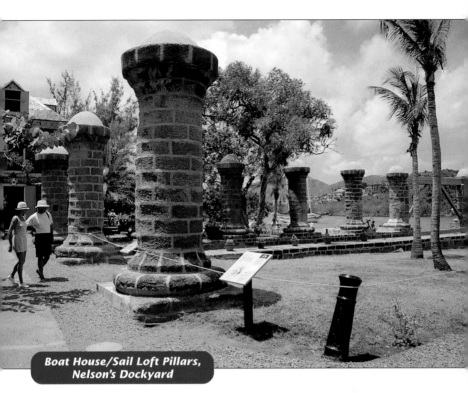

Boat House/Sail Loft Pillars, Nelson's Dockyard

communities that falls within the 15-square mile (39-sq km) national park area which also encompasses Nelson's Dockyard, English Harbour and Shirley Heights. Other communities within the park are **English Harbour** and **Cobb's Cross**, which is why the national park is also called The Living Park.

Fort Charles on **Blake Island** in Falmouth Harbour is one of the oldest forts on Antigua. It was built in 1672 and extended in 1714 when it had a battery of fourteen cannon.

Cobbs Cross is noted for its egret colony, and flights of these graceful white birds make spectacular sunrises and sunsets even more stunning.

English Harbour Town is separated from Falmouth by a small neck of land. English Harbour is even more protected than Falmouth

Harbour, and this was quickly appreciated by the Royal Navy who chose it as a site for a naval dockyard. It had many advantages: it offered a safe, deep water anchorage, the headlands protected sheltering vessels from hurricanes, and the Harbour and approaches could be easily defended.

These forts included **Fort Berkeley**, built to protect the western approaches. The fort was started in 1704 and extended and strengthened on several occasions over the next fifty years. It eventually had twenty-nine cannon. A nature trail leads to the Fort.

Nelson's Dockyard

Nelson's Dockyard is one of the most historic dockyards in the world, and one of the safest. Over the centuries it has been used by pirates and privateers, and during the Napoleonic Wars it provided a safe haven for British Royal Navy ships when they were not harassing French vessels. Work on the dockyard started in 1743 and continued for almost a hundred years as more refinements were added until it became one of the most important naval bases in the Caribbean, and the headquarters of the Royal Navy's powerful East Caribbean fleet.

Over the years, the dockyard has played host to some of Britain's most famous seafarers, including Admirals (Horatio) Nelson, Rodney and Hood. Admiral Lord Rodney is famous for his victory over the French fleet under de Grasse off Dominica during the American Revolution; Admiral Viscount Samuel Hood was a brilliant naval strategist who thwarted the French invasion of British St Kitts and Nevis, and later blockaded most of the French navy inside their base at Toulon in the Mediterranean for four months.

Nelson's Dockyard is now important as the world's last Georgian dockyard, and is protected as part of a national park area, although the Harbour and year-round marina now teems with luxury yachts rather than fighting ships. The eighteenth century quay and its buildings have been well restored and the area can have changed little over the last 200 years.

The stone warehouses, boat houses, blacksmith's, sawpits, sail loft with its massive pillars which took 15 months to build and garrison quarters are now home to shops, boutiques, inns and restaurants. The **Officers Quarters** is built over

The Copper & Lumber Store, Nelson's Dockyard

a massive underground cistern which stored water. Officers lived in the building while their ships lay at anchor during the hurricane system. There is now an art gallery upstairs.

The original **Copper and Lumber Store**, with its unique Georgian arched courtyard, is now a delightful hotel. Originally copper was beaten on to the hulls of wooden ships to strengthen them, while the timber was needed for repairs. The huge stone bollards that were used to moor the men-o'-wars, still stand proudly along the water's edge.

The dockyard's main purpose was to act as a careening station for vessels. The ships' bottoms would be covered in barnacles and scratches after crossing the Atlantic. Having reached the shelter of the quay, the ships would be pulled on to their sides using ropes attached to massive capstans, so that the sailors could clean the exposed bottom and repaint and repair them. The capstans have been restored and stand at the water's edge.

The **Admiral's House**, where Nelson stayed briefly in 1805 while a senior captain, is now the **Dockyard Museum** with exhibits chronicling the history and work of the dockyard, and some of its famous visitors. Despite its name,

English Harbour

there is no evidence that any admiral ever lived in the house. By the museum stands an old sandbox tree which is at least 200 years old. It derives its name from the large pods filled with sand which the officers kept on their desks to sprinkle over wet ink to help it dry. Behind the building is the old stone kitchen and the ancient ovens are still in use by the bakery.

Clarence House was built in 1787 on the hillside opposite the dockyard, and this was where

Prince William Henry, Duke of Clarence and captain of the *HMS Pegasus*, stayed when in dock. A close friend of Nelson, a fellow Captain, he later became King William IV, and other members of the British Royal Family have since been guests there. Clarence House is now the official country home of the Governor-General. When he is not in residence, this Georgian house, complete with period furnishings, is open to the public.

The dockyard played a vital strategic role in Britain's retaining her Caribbean colonies during the nineteenth century, but as European nations made peace there was less need for a strong naval presence in the Caribbean.

Emancipation and the extensive use of sugar beet in Europe also hit the profitability of the sugar cane plantations, so the need to protect this trade diminished. These two factors brought about the demise of the dockyards and it was closed in 1889.

The area fell into disrepair but in 1951 an adventurous restoration agenda was initiated as part of a joint scheme between the Antigua and Barbuda National Parks Authority and the Canadian International Development Agency, and ten years later it re-opened rather ironically as Nelson's Dockyard. Although Nelson spent three years based at or sailing from the dockyard, he was not overly fond of it,

Dow's Hill

Dow's Hill overlooks English Harbour and is the home of the new **Interpretation Centre** ☎ 460-2777. There are great views from the hilltop over the sites of the first European settlements established in the early seventeenth century, and the fortifications around English Harbour.

The Centre, named after General Alexander Dow, who commanded the Shirley Heights garrison, has been cleverly built incorporating old fortifications. The Centre's highlight is a multi-media presentation called *Reflections of the Sun*. The presentation has been designed so that as you view the various tableaux, the history of the islands unfolds around you, from the first Amerindian settlers, through the Plantocracy, British military period and the freedom struggle to Emancipation and beyond.

The nearby **Belvedere** is built on what remains of the eighteenth century Governor-General's residence. The house was destroyed by an earthquake in 1843 although its foundations and those of the outbuildings can still be seen. From its breathtaking vantage point the Belvedere offers true panoramic views, and the interpretative panels to help you pick out important landmarks.

Also at Dow's Hill is the entrance to **Batcave**. It is on the campus of the medical school, and there are tours of the cave accompanied by a fascinating discourse on island folklore. According to legend there is an undersea tunnel running from the cave all the way to Guadeloupe, and this was supposedly used as an escape route by runaway slaves.

The Lookout, Shirley Heights

and described it variously in his diaries and letters, as 'this vile spot' and 'this barbarous island'. He was stationed at the dockyard between 1784 and 1787 as Captain of the frigate *HMS Boreas* and his disillusionment with Antigua was due in part of his having to enforce the Navigation Act, which outlawed the islanders' lucrative trade with passing American ships. The Act also annoyed the British colonial officers on the island who had turned a blind eye to the trade and profited from it.

While based on Antigua, however, Nelson met Frances 'Fanny' Nesbit, a young widow from nearby St Kitts. He met her in March 1785 and married her on Nevis two years later, returning to England with her and her young son immediately afterwards. Prince William Henry acted as best man. Nelson returned to the dockyard briefly in 1805 as Admiral in charge of the British fleet chasing the French, a confrontation which ended in both his victory and death at the Battle of Trafalgar, off the Spanish coast on

21 October of that year.

Today Nelson's Dockyard and surrounding park is delightful, and makes a fascinating visit. There is a **Visitors' Centre** (☎ 460-1053) plus shops and boutiques, hotels and restaurants – and nearby, of course, beautiful beaches .

It is worth exploring the peninsula on which Nelson's Dockyard stands. At the southern tip is **Snapper Point,** a barren area with cacti.

Indian Creek is another important site because archaeological excavations suggest it is the site of the first Amerindian settlement within the national park. Arawak and Carib relics have been unearthed.

This is a great area for exploring the rich marine life that teems in the inshore waters protected by the coral reef.

Shirley Heights

Shirley Heights is south of the Interpretation Centre and offers a delightful walk through the woods, and an insight into how strongly fortified the area was. The Heights are littered with the remains of old gun emplacements, batteries, powder magazines and barracks of **Fort Shirley**. The area is named after General Sir Thomas Shirley, who was appointed Governor of the Leeward Islands in 1781 and served for ten years. He immediately set about building fortifications around the island, and the massive Fort Shirley took ten years to complete. There is a small museum in the area known as the Royal Artillery Quarters, which traces the history and development of the fort.

The Lookout Trail winds through the Shirley Heights Forest with its red barked turpentine trees, cinnamon and loblolly trees. The leaves of the loblolly were used to make a tea which was given as a purgative, and this led nineteenth century Royal Navy sailors to call any ship's medicine 'loblolly'. The **Shirley Heights Lookout** has been built incorporating some of the old military remains, and offers wonderful views across English Harbour and the surrounding fortifications. It is easy to see how effective the cannon would have been in protecting the seaward approaches from attack.

A late afternoon tradition every Sunday, and now Thursday as well, is for tourists and locals alike to gather to watch the fabulous sunset to the sounds of a steel band, and then enjoy a barbecue and drinks including local rum. An intriguing mix of old and new greets you as you look out over the old naval dockyard with its centuries-old traditions, while listening to the pulsating rhythms of the drummers and the latest reggae hits. You can also get to Shirley Heights along Fig Tree Drive.

Blockhouse Hill

Situated on Cape Shirley, over 400 feet (122m) above the sea, Blockhouse Hill derives its name from the fortified structures built on the crest. These include gun emplacements, powder stores, water cisterns and barracks, and the blockhouse, built in 1787. It was designed as the place for last resistance in case of attack, but was largely used as officers' quarters.

Close by is the old military cemetery which has an obelisk commemorating soldiers of the 54th Regiment who died during a yellow fever outbreak between 1848 and 1851. The Shirley Heights garrison was withdrawn in 1854 when the troops were dispatched to fight in the Crimea, and it was never manned again.

The Friends of English Harbour are now preserving the area around Charlotte Peninsula, the site of the Carpenter family home dating back to 1750. The huge sandstone pillars rising from the sea below Shirley Heights are known locally as the Pillars of Hercules.

Mamora Bay is popular with scuba divers and snorkels because of the Mamora Reef which is noted for its beautiful corals.

Back to St John's

Follow the coast road round **Willoughby Bay** through Christian Hill to Bethesda, and then round

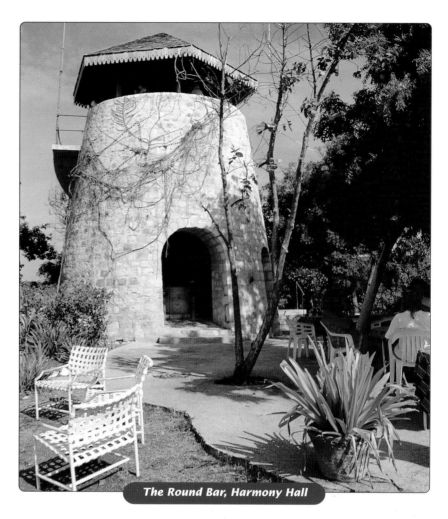

The Round Bar, Harmony Hall

the head of the bay to **Fort William**, with the Horse Shoe Reef offshore.

Half Moon Bay is considered by many to be the island's most beautiful beach, but there are many other rivals. The shape of the bay and its exposure to the Atlantic means that it can be affected by a wide range of different conditions along the beach, with some areas experiencing only a gentle swell while others having crashing surf. There is a stables close to the beach if you fancy a horse ride through the surf. Also nearby is the Half Moon Bay Hotel and golf course.

Exchange Bay is the home of the Mill Reef Club.

You have to retrace your route, then head north through **Freetown**, so named because it was founded by freed slaves after Emancipation in 1834, to **Harmony Hall**, which looks out over Nonsuch Bay. The Hall, originally the Great House of Brown's Bay Mill, is built round an old sugar mill. The mill now houses a round bar and has an observation deck that offers fabulous views. There is also a restaurant and a beach nearby where you can have a swim. More importantly,

Harmony Hall features the work of local artists and craftsmen in an art gallery and studios, and stages an annual craft fair. It is open daily from 10am to 6pm ☎ 460-4120.

Again, retrace your route to the main road, turn right, then left at the T-junction. Pass the service station on your left and skirt the **Potworks Dam Reservoir** to the north, and then take the secondary road on your left through Freemans, heading west to connect with the main road back to St John's.

TOUR 2 — The North

Drive north out of St John's, turn left at the Barrymore Hotel and then keep on the roads which follow the sea. The road runs out at Fort James.

This stretch of coastline north of St John's is the most heavily developed on the island with many hotels looking out over **Runaway Bay** and **Dickenson Bay** where there are the remains of another of the island's defensive network of eighteenth century forts. This is also a popular area for wealthy Antiguans to build their large, luxury homes.

The coast runs north past Weatherills Point and Soldier Point to **Boon Point,** the northernmost tip of the island. Follow the coast road round through Cedar Grove to Hodges Bay, which has a number of resort hotels and also boasts the island's oldest house although it is not open to the public. It is an old Great House dating from the early seventeenth century. The road continues to **Beggar's Point,** another

Fort James

The fort was built on the headland, overlooking St John's, between 1704 and 1706 on the site of a 1670s fortification. It was named in 1734 after King James II and its purpose was to protect St John's Harbour and the sea approaches from attacks by pirates, especially French corsairs, from nearby Guadeloupe to the south.

Extended in the 1740s and again in 1773 its massive walls that have survived the centuries date from about 1740. The fort's weaponry was increased to thirty-six cannon during the American Revolution, and although never fired in anger, one was fired each day at sun-up and sundown, and whenever a visiting warship arrived.

Today there are ten or so of these huge cannon, each weighing more than two tons (2000kg), to add to the atmosphere and your photographs. Each massive cannon needed a gun crew of twelve men. The fort is worth visiting both for the history and the tremendous views.

area with hotels and restaurants and the Gambles Golf Course. On Sandy Lane, behind the Hodges Bay Club, is Aiton Place, the home and studio of artist and film maker Nick Maley. He also has a gallery on Heritage Quay.

The road then runs south along the coast past Shoal Point and the island's defense regiment base to Barnacle Point, with Maiden Island offshore and low lying **Long Island** just beyond. Long Island was once used for raising cattle, which explains why its northern promontory is called Pasture Point. Today it is the home of the Jumby Bay Resort, for those who really want to get away from it all. Guests land at the international airport and are then ferried across to their own tropical island.

The road then runs inland towards the VC Bird International Airport, but take the secondary road along the coast with Fitches Creek inland and Fitches Creek Bay on your left. Continue on the secondary road to **Parham**, one of the oldest settlements on the island and although many claim it used to be the capital, this is not the case.

St Peter's Anglican Church

This unusual octagonal Italianate church in Parnham was designed by Thomas Weekes and built in the 1840s to replace the original 1711 wooden church which burned down, and the 1754 replace-ment which was dismantled to make way for the new building. It has recently been restored and is noted for its ribbed wooden ceiling and the crafts-manship of the masonry. It has been described as the finest church in the British West Indies and it still has some of the original stucco work.

The Arch, Devil's Bridge

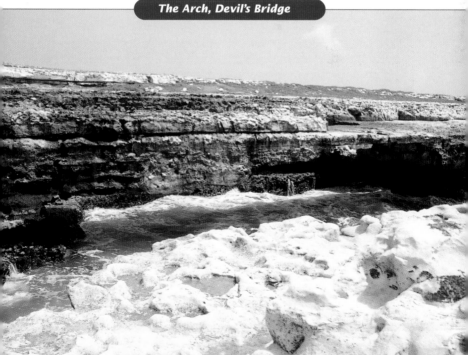

There are still a number of old buildings and traditional clapboard houses nestling among the palms close to the water and a fort still stands guard over the town and waters beyond.

North of Parham Harbour is Fitches Creek which has another charming little church. **St George's Church** was built in the late 1680s, although extensively rebuilt in the 1730s and again at the beginning of the twentieth century. It contains the marble scroll from the grave of the first English settler to be buried in a place of worship on the island in 1659. Part of its charm lies in its setting which looks out over spectacular seascapes.

You can explore Crabs Peninsula with Guiana Island just offshore. Then return to Parham and head south on the main road, turning left for Pares and continuing east through Glanvilles and Willikies to visit **Indian Town National Park**. The park lies on a narrow peninsula that juts out into the sea and takes the full force of the Atlantic rollers which crash in. These waves have carved out the **Devil's Bridge**, a natural arch formed by the erosion of the soft limestone.

There are also several blowholes in the surrounding rocks. Blowholes are usually formed as a result of the continuous action of the water carving out a tunnel or cave in a stratum of soft rock. When the end of the tunnel collapses water shoots along it and then explodes out and upwards through the blowhole. The intensity of the blow out obviously depends on the strength of the surf. It's great fun trying to click the camera just at the right moment to capture the event on film.

Betty's Hope

Journey back in time to Antigua's first large-scale sugar estate. Betty's Hope was established in 1650 by Governor Christopher Keynell. The owners fled when the French occupied the island for six months in 1666, and in 1674 the estate was taken over by Sir Christopher Codrington, and named after his daughter. It remained in the Codrington family for almost 300 years. In effect, Betty's Hope was the seat of Government for the whole of the Leeward Islands as successive members of the Codrington family served as Governor-General from the late seventeenth century until some way into the eighteenth century.

There are many old ruins and remains, and of special interest are the twin towers of the wind-driven sugar mills, and the arches that supported the boiling house. The sugar mill is the only working, authentic windmill in the Caribbean and the crushing mill was supplied

Arawak relics have been found in this area, so there may have been early settlements here.

Retrace your route towards Pares but turn off left and follow the signs to **Betty's Hope**.

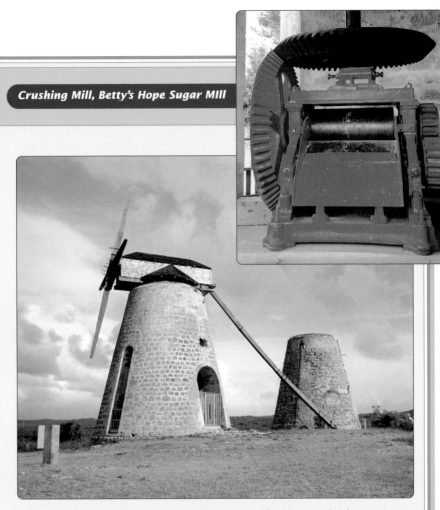

in the mid-nineteenth century by Fletchers of Derby, England. The original machinery had all been removed after the mill fell into disrepair, and the restoration team had to scour Antigua and surrounding islands for replacement parts and then had to figure out how to reconstruct a nineteenth-century working mill.

The estate, now operated by the Betty's Hope Trust, is open to the public from Tuesday to Saturday, and is well sign-posted.

Back to St John's

Head back to the main road, turn left and continue through Pares to the T-junction. Turn right and then left again at Vernons, for the road back into St John's through Potters Village and St Johnston Village.

You can take a small detour south on the road opposite the abandoned sugar factory to **Sea View Farm**, a traditional pottery village where pots are still made from local clay.

• BARBUDA •

Barbuda lies 30 miles (49km) north of Antigua and offers some of the finest, longest natural beaches in the Caribbean while the heavily wooded hinterland – with the Highlands in the north rising to 130 feet (40m) above the sea – is a naturalist's paradise. Barbuda also boasts the best-tasting lobster in the Caribbean.

Getting around Barbuda

By air

Barbuda is only a twenty-minute hop from Antigua and makes a great day out if you can't stay for longer. LIAT flies from Antigua daily at 8.15am and 3.30pm, while flights from Barbuda leave at 8.45am and 4pm.

Carib Aviation also flies charters to Barbuda, tailored to suit your special needs.

By sea

Boats can be chartered for the four-hour crossing from Antigua, and a number of companies offer boats, either crewed or bare-board (see yachting section in the FactFile).

By car

The best way to get around is by car although there is only a handful available for rent. Passing cars will stop to give you a lift but the roads are not exactly busy.

Other ways to see the island are by foot, or by taking a boat to reach secluded beaches, the bird reserve and so on.

Reefs lie off the north, east and south-east coasts, and there are extensive marshes in the southern part of the inland. The Highlands contain many caves, most of which have not been thoroughly explored.

The Codrington lease

Poor soil excluded Barbuda from intensive sugar cane cultivation and consequently the island was used largely for rearing livestock. This accounts for many of the place names, such as Goat Island, Goat Point, Billy Point, Rabbit Island, Hog Point and so on. In 1685 King Charles II granted the Codrington family a fifty-year lease in return for a peppercorn rent of 'one fat sheep'. The family retained their lease until 1870 even though the island had been officially ceded to Antigua ten years earlier. Apart from the land, the family had rights to 'all wreckage' and as there were many shipwrecks on the offshore reefs, this boosted their fortunes considerably. There are still lots of goats, and agriculture and fishing are the main industries.

In the old days the islanders supplemented their income as wreckers. Lights would be erected on a promontory so that passing ships would be tricked into thinking they were close to a settlement. The ships would head for the coast and founder on the reefs where their freight would be salvaged by the waiting islanders.

Most of the island's population lives in the main settlement of **Codrington Village**, a collection of clapboard houses and a handful of streets.

The village is on Codrington Lagoon, the largest lagoon in the Caribbean which teems with fish and the famous Barbuda lobsters.

The main airstrip is just to the south of Codrington Village. There is a second airstrip servicing the exclusive Coco Point Lodge in the south-east corner of the island in its own secluded 164 acres (66 hectares). The 1,200 islanders rely heavily on the sea for their living, and it is said that there are more turtles on the island than locals.

Visitors love Barbuda for its very laid-back atmosphere, the stunning beaches and world-class diving and snorkeling. The longest stretch of beach extends for 7 miles (11km) and at certain times of the year the sand takes on a pink hue, the result of millions of tiny pieces of crushed coral and shell being washed ashore.

Over the last three centuries many ships have foundered on the offshore reefs which enclose the island, and the seventy-three charted sites offer excellent dives. Scuba equipment is not available on Barbuda outside the two resorts, although Antiguan dive operators run trips to the resorts.

Barbuda

The Magnificent Frigate bird

The sanctuary, on an area of Codrington Lagoon overgrown with squat mangroves, is home to the magnificent frigate bird, and is best reached by launch. It is the largest colony of these birds in the Lesser Antilles. The birds, which have a wingspan of up to 90 inches (2.3m), are often called man o' war birds, because they are, in every sense, hunters of the ocean. The birds can catch fish close to the surface but, remarkably for birds that spend most of their life over the water, their feathers are not waterproof; if their plumage gets wet they cannot fly. Because of this, the birds cannot dive into the water to catch fish so they have become pirates, swooping on other birds to make them drop their catches which are then caught in mid air. On Barbuda the birds are not disturbed by humans and are almost tame.

The frigatebird can be spotted by its long forked tail, pointed wings, streamlined silhouette and vicious curved bill. It soars effortlessly on the wind and its habit of opening and closing its tail feathers for direction changes gives it the Caribbean patois name of 'siso' (scissors).The adult male is black and has a scarlet throat pouch which is inflated like a balloon during courtship rituals, while the female has a white breast and sides. The young of both sexes have white heads and breasts. A single egg is laid in a crude nest of sticks and the young bird is dependent on its mother for at least a year.

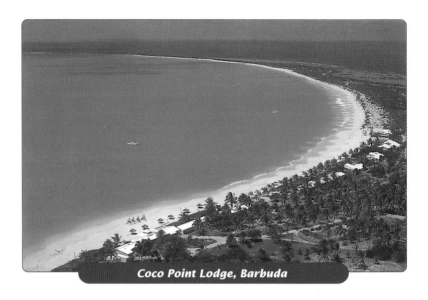

Coco Point Lodge, Barbuda

The beaches around the island are also great for beachcombing, you never know what may be washed up from one of the wreck sites!

For naturalists there are the Highland woods which are home to wild pig and fallow deer, introduced by the Codrington family and allowed to roam free.

The lagoons and mangrove swamps, as well as the bird sanctuary on the north-west coast, are the places for bird watchers.

A limited number of seasonal deer hunting licences are available from the police station in Codrington Village. Other game includes blue wing teal, white cheeks, pigeons and guinea fowl.

Places to visit

There are several **caves** in the northern Highlands part of the island, most of which remain unexplored although several of those that have bear petroglyphs carved by Arawaks. Dark Cave, inland from Two Feet Bay, is at least 300 feet (91m) deep, while inland between Pigeon Cliff and Castle Bay is the Darby Sink Cave – 300 feet (91m) across and 80 feet (24m) deep.

Highland House, situated at the highest point on the island, was built by the Codrington family in 1750 as their official home on the island, but it was seldom used as they preferred to stay on Antigua. It has long since fallen into ruins with only a few walls and some shells of outbuildings remaining, mostly covered by vines and other vegetation.

The **River Fort Martello Tower** is on the south coast and was built to protect the island's original quay. The 56-foot-high (15m) tower remains although the nine cannon which were mounted on the gun emplacement on top have long since gone.

Palaster Reef off the south-east coast is a National Marine Park. The most southerly part of the island is **Spanish Point** with the remains of the Spanish Point Tower, often called the Castle. Nearby, Amerindian sites have been found dating back 2,000 years. There are two exclusive resorts – the K Club and Coco Point Lodge, although more modest accommodation is also available.

• REDONDA •

This uninhabited rock is one of the strangest and smallest 'kingdoms' in the world. In 1865 an Irishman, Matthew Shiell, who lived on Montserrat, and happened to be sailing past, 'claimed' the tiny island for his son Philippe, who passed it on to the poet John Gawsworth. He declared himself King Juan I, and dispensed aristocratic titles on his literary friends, including J.B. Priestley, Dylan Thomas and Rebecca West.

People did live on the island in the second half of the nineteenth century, mining the guano – bird droppings that had accumulated over thousands of years from the huge colonies of nesting birds. The guano was shipped out as a plant food.

There was once a tiny post office on the island and Redonda stamps are rare and highly collectible.

The current 'king' resides in Sussex, and his thousands of 'subjects' are made up of seabirds, lizards and a few goats. The only way to see Redonda is to charter a boat to take you there.

Bird life

Today the island still attracts bird watchers for its many different species of seabirds and particularly for the burrowing owl which is now extinct on Antigua. The owl is easily distinguishable from other owls because of its long legs, which give it added height when on the ground. It is nocturnal, nests in pairs or small colonies, and often perches in the entrance to its burrow during the day. It has developed a mechanism to defend itself when disturbed in its burrow – it imitates the sound of a rattlesnake.

Note: Most restaurants, but not all, accept credit cards, so check first.

$$ Abracadabra, Nelson's Dockyard, English Harbour, Italian. Try the delicious home-made pasta and fresh lobster. There is a popular video bar with live reggae music on Tuesday, a band on Thursday, and DJ every Friday and Saturday. Open nightly ☎ 460-1732.

$$-$$$ The Admiral's Inn, Nelson's Dockyard, West Indian and International. Dine in the historic Georgian Inn or outside under the trees with stunning views over English Harbour. Open daily for breakfast, lunch and dinner. Closed September. Reservations recommended ☎ 460-1027.

$$-$$$ Alberto's, Willoughby Bay, Italian. Open for dinner in the charming gazebo, with seafood and Italian dishes, accompanied by great wines. You can even tour the wine cellar to select your own bottle. It is open nightly except Monday and closed over the summer. Reservations recommended ☎ 460-3007.

$$-$$$ Al Porto Ristorante and Bar, Jolly Harbour, Italian. A lively restaurant offering pizzas, pastas and seafood and open air dining. The restaurant is open daily from 10am to late, and happy hour is from 6pm to 7pm each evening ☎ 462-7695.

$-$$ Alibi Restaurant and Sports Bar, Lower Redcliffe Quay, St John's ☎ 462-7936.

$ Aly's Roti and Grill Shop, 20 Long Street, St John's, Caribbean ☎ 460-7684.

$$ Ambassador, Sunset Cove Resort, seafood and International.

$$$ The Andes Restaurant and Bar, Royal Antiguan National Resort, seafood and Caribbean. The restaurant overlooks Deep Bay and is named after a ship that sank there in 1907. Great seafood and steaks and nightly entertainment by reggae, calypso and jazz groups. There is a Wednesday night barbecue and Friday night Caribbean buffet. It is open for lunch and dinner daily ☎ 462-3733.

$$ Bon Appetit, Church Street, St John's, International ☎ 462-6424

$-$$$ Brown Sugar Restaurant, Antigua Sugar Mill Hotel, International and West Indian. A lovely restaurant open all day for snacks, full meals and tempting desserts, and romantic dinners with the freshest of seafood. Happy Hour is from 5pm to 7pm every night. The next door Sugar Lofty Cocktail Lounge is open daily from 7am to 11.30pm ☎ 462-0857.

$-$$ **Catherine's Cafe**,
Antigua Slipway, Island fare,
☎ 460-5050.

$-$$ **China Restaurant**,
St Mary's Street, St John's,
Chinese. Authentic Chinese
cuisine served Monday to
Saturday from 11.30am to
11pm and on Sunday from
6.30pm to 11pm ☎ 461-6463.

$$-$$$ **Coconut Grove
Beach Restaurant**,
Dickenson Beach,
International. A delightful
award-winning 'tropical'
restaurant by the water with
palm trees for shade. Open
daily for breakfast, lunch and
dinner and noted for its
seafood and wide range of
exotic cocktails ☎ 462-1538.

$$-$$$ **Colombo's**,
Galleon Beach Club, English
Harbour, Italian. The
restaurant is named after
Columbus' landing place, so it
is appropriate that there is an
Italian restaurant on the site.
Excellent authentic Italian
cooking featuring home-made
pastas, lobster and veal
specials, with the added
bonuses of wonderful scenery
and a relaxed atmosphere. It
is open daily for lunch and
dinner ☎ 460-1452.

$-$$ **Crazy Cactus Cantina**,
All Saint's Road, close to
St John's, Antigua's first
Mexican restaurant. Both the
atmosphere and the food are
spicy. Good value. Open for
lunch and dinner daily except
Monday ☎ 462-1183.

$$$ **Curtain Bluff
Restaurant**, Curtain Bluff
Hotel, Old Road, Morris Bay,
International. Fine dining in a
charming atmosphere and
noted for both its seafood
dishes and superb wine list.
The wine cellar has 25,000
bottles. The restaurant is
open daily for lunch and
dinner Monday to Saturday
between mid-October and
mid-May. Dinner reservations
are necessary and men are
expected to wear jacket and
tie ☎ 462-8400.

$-$$ **The Deck**, English
Harbour, West Indian. A lively
place to enjoy good value
snacks and well-prepared
West Indian dishes and
seafood. For a real treat pop
down for a traditional West
Indian Sunday breakfast.
There is a cocktail bar and
disco, and happy hour is from
6pm to 7pm. The restaurant
is open from 8am to late
☎ 460-1719.

$$ **The Docksider**,
St James's Club, Mamora Bay,
seafood and West Indian.
Open for casually elegant
dining. Reservations
recommended ☎ 460-5000.

$-$$ **Fandango Bar and
Restaurant**, Falmouth,
seafood and local dishes
☎460-1725.

$-$$ **Fisherman's Wharf**,
Heritage Quay, St John's,
West Indian and seafood.
A popular waterfront eatery
where you can refuel after
exploring the town or simply

enjoy the quay views and the good West Indian food and snacks. It is open from 11am on Monday to Saturday and from 6pm on Sunday. Happy hour is from 6pm to 7pm. Take out and delivery are available ☎ 462-2248.

$$-$$$ Harmony Hall, Freetown, seafood and Caribbean. The views over Nonsuch Bay from the round bar in the sugar mill are tremendous, as is the seafood offered at lunch and dinner. The lobster is wonderful. The restaurant is open daily from 10am to 6pm and snacks are served during the afternoon. Apart from the food, the place is worth visiting for the displays of Caribbean arts and crafts which can, of course, be purchased ☎ 460-4120.

$$$ Hawksbill Beach Resort, Five Islands, West Indian and Continental. Casually elegant dining inside or on the terrace. Breakfast and dinner are taken in the restaurant, with lunch offered in the beach restaurant ☎ 462-0301.

$$ Hemingway's, St Mary's Street, St John's, West Indian and International. Dine out on the deck which catches the gentle breeze, and enjoy great seafood and island dishes. It is open Monday to Saturday from 8.30am ☎ 462-2763.

$$-$$$ The Inn at English Harbour, West Indian and International. A great place for a meal at any time of the day, but especially if you want a romantic dinner. Dining on the terrace by candlelight, with the yachts bobbing in the water and Nelson's Dockyard and Freeman's Bay as the backdrop, is a truly memorable occasion. The à la carte menu changes daily to ensure only the freshest of produce is served, and outstanding dishes include seafood, Thai curries and West Indian dishes. The restaurant is open daily but closed from early September to mid-October ☎ 460-1014.

$ Jacinta's Restaurant and Snack Shop, Lower Market Square, West Indian. A really good place to try authentic island dishes such as ducana and saltfish, rice with side dishes, fungi and saltfish, and the ever-bubbling pepper pot. It is open Monday to Saturday from 6am to 5pm. No telephone.

$$-$$$ La Perruche, English Harbour, French and West Indian. Romantic, fine dining either in the elegant restaurant or by candlelight in the garden. Impressive wine list. Open Monday to Saturday from 7pm to 10.30pm. Reservations recommended ☎ 460-3040.

$$$ Le Bistro, Hodges Bay, French and International. Fine dining for those who truly appreciate it. Wonderful seafood creations, memorable sauces and a bill to match, but worth every cent. Open for dinner Tuesday to Sunday ☎ 462-3881.

$$-$$$ Le Cap Horn, English Harbour, French and Argentinean. Great beef, seafood and lobster and tempting desserts. Open daily from 6.30pm to 11pm ☎ 460-1194.

$$-$$$ The Lemon Tree, Long Street, St John's, International. A popular night-club-style restaurant with live music and late night relaxing. Open Monday to Friday for lunch and dinner from 10.30am to late, and dinner only on Saturday ☎ 462-1969.

$$ Limey's, Nelson's Dockyard, West Indian. Tasty West Indian dishes, freshly-baked pastries and a wide range of refreshing island fruit juices and other drinks. Happy hour is from 3pm to 5pm. Open daily from 8am to 10pm ☎ 460-1144.

$$ Mango Bay Lagoon Restaurant, Dian Bay, seafood and International ☎ 460-6646.

$$-$$$ The Orchid, Royal Antiguan Renaissance, Oriental. Elegant dining Tuesday, Thursday and weekends. Reservations recommended ☎ 462-3733,

$$-$$$ Paco Rabanne, Jolly Harbour, dine in style aboard one of the world's largest and most luxurious yachts. The all-inclusive price includes buffet dinner, rum punch, entertainment and dancing. There is even a casino on board. Reservations recommended ☎ 462-6210.

$$-$$$ Pascal's, St James' Club, excellent French restaurant. Reservations recommended ☎ 460-5000.

$$ The Rookery, Blue Heron Hotel, Johnsons Point, West Indian, French and International. Intimate, gracious dining with à la carte and table d'hôte menus, with Creole buffet, steel band and live entertainment popular weekly features. Open daily from 7pm to 9.30pm ☎ 462-8564.

$$-$$$ Shirley Heights Lookout, Shirley Heights, West Indian and seafood. Dine in style with magnificent views over Nelson's Dockyard. Steel band concert accompanies the Thursday 3.30pm to 8pm barbecue, and the Sunday barbecue features six hours of live entertainment from 3pm to 9pm ☎ 460-1785.

$$-$$$ Spinnaker's Beach Bar and Restaurant, Dickenson Bay, Continental and West Indian. Good seafood, steaks and daily specials. Great place for sunset watching with cocktail in hand. Open daily from 7.30am to late. Happy hour is from 5pm to 7pm with live entertainment most nights. Reservations recommended ☎ 462-4158.

ARRIVAL, ENTRY REQUIREMENTS AND CUSTOMS

Visitors who are citizens of Canada and the United States and not planning to stay for more than six months, must produce one of the following: valid passport, birth certificate, Citizenship Card or Nationalisation Certificate, or Voter's Registration Card. Visitors from Britain, the European Union, Australia and Japan require a valid passport while most other visitors require a visa, so check with your travel company. You may also be asked to show a return air ticket, and evidence of pre-arranged accommodation and adequate means of support. An immigration form has to be filled in and presented on arrival. The form requires you to say where you will be staying on the island, and if you plan to move around, put down the first hotel you will be staying at. The immigration form is in two parts, one of which is stamped and returned to you in your passport. You must retain this until departure when the slip is retrieved as you check in at the airport.

If visiting on business, a letter confirming this may prove helpful in speeding your way through customs, especially if you are carrying samples.

Having cleared immigration you will have to go through customs, and it is quite usual to have to open your luggage for inspection. If you have expensive cameras, electrical goods, etc it is a good idea to travel with photocopies of the receipts.

When entering Antigua your duty-free allowance is 200 cigarettes, 50 cigars or 250g (9oz) of tobacco, 1 litre/liter of spirits or wine and 170ml (6oz) of perfume.

ACCOMMODATION

There is a wide range of accommodation to suit all tastes and pockets, from top class hotels to delightful guest-houses, self-catering apartments, luxury villas and beach cottages. There are about 4,200 hotel rooms on Antigua and Barbuda, with a total of 6,500 beds. Almost all hotels and apartments are close to or on the beach, most rooms are air conditioned or have ceiling fans, and most properties offer a wide range of sports and entertainment.

If you want to eat out and explore quite a lot it pays to stay in a hotel offering board only. If you want to laze on the beach and not stray far from the hotel, choose a hotel package offering meals as well.

There are also apartments, holiday villas and beach cottages available for short and long rent offering you the privacy of your own accommodation and the flexibility to eat in or out, with cooks and maid service available if required. The 'high season' runs from mid-December to mid-April and prices tend to be lower at other times. There are no youth hostel or camping facilities on the islands.

Some terms

AI	—	All inclusive
MAP	—	Modified American Plan (breakfast and dinner are included)
EP	—	European Plan (bed only and no meals)
AP	—	American Plan (room and all meals)

Prices quoted by hotels are for rooms, whether one or two people are sharing, and you may find it difficult to get a reduction if you are visit alone, but have a go. $ represents inexpensive accommodation, $$ moderate, and $$$ de-luxe.

Antigua

HOTELS

$$ EP Admiral's Inn,
English Harbour. A delightful, restored Georgian weathered brick building dating from 1788, with huge hand-hewn beams in the heart of Nelson's Dockyard National Park ☎ 460-1153/1027 Fax 460-1534.

$$$ AI Allegro Pineapple Beach Club,
Long Bay. Situated in a secluded 25-acre (10-hectare) lush setting along a lovely beach. The all-inclusive resort has 135 rooms with two restaurants, bar, pool, tennis, nightly live entertainment, walking trails, snorkeling, windsurfing and instruction, and watersports ☎ 463-2006/800 858 2258 Fax 463-2452.

$$ EP Antigua Sugar Mill Hotel,
Coolidge. Serves as the airport hotel. It has 24 air-conditioned rooms and large swimming pool set in the lush tropical gardens. There is a restaurant and fabulous views of the Caribbean from the observation deck over the round bar in the 260-year-old sugar mill ☎ 462-1455 Fax 462-1534.

$$-$$$ EP Antigua Village,
Dickenson Bay, is a delightful Mediterranean-style villa development 2 miles (3km) from St John's, and 5 miles (8km) from the airport. Set in lovely tropical gardens beside the sea, it offers 56 air-conditioned studios and one and two-bedroom apartments, all with kitchens ☎ 462-2930 Fax 462-0375.

$$ Blue Waters,
set in magnificent tropical gardens on its own private bay with two white sand beaches. It has 77 rooms and suites and one to three bedroom beachside villas. Facilities include two restaurants – the open air Palm Restaurant and the à la carte Vyvian's Restaurant – bars, beauty spa, watersports, snorkeling with nearby golf, casinos and discos ☎ 462-0290 Fax 462-0293.

$ EP Catamaran Hotel and Marina,
Falmouth Harbour, offers 16 waterside rooms close to Nelson's Dockyard. Facilities include restaurant and bar, sunfish, rowing boats, snorkeling and deep sea fishing ☎ 460-1506.

$$$ Club Antigua, Lignumvitae Bay, is 12 miles (19km) from the airport and 7 miles (11km) from St John's. The all-inclusive resort has 464 rooms and 6 villas set in 40 acres (16 hectares) of tropical gardens on the one mile (1.6km) long Jolly Beach. It offers 4 restaurants and 6 bars, mini casino, pool, floodlit tennis, children's club, disco, live entertainment nightly, daily activities, free bikes, scuba sailing and watersports. There are also wedding and honeymoon packages ☎ 462-0061 (UK 01372-466944, US 1-800-777-1250) Fax 462-4900.

$$-$$$ CoCo's Antigua, set on a bluff between two beaches and overlooking Jolly Bay. There are six spacious gingerbread cottages, an award winning restaurant, watersports, snorkeling, and nearby tennis, squash, golf, shopping and restaurants ☎ 460-2626 Fax 462-9423.

$$$ EP Copper and Lumber Store Hotel, English Harbour. The hotel offers 13 studios and suites in a lovely old building set in well tended gardens. There is a boat shuttle to nearby beaches. The Wardroom restaurant is noted for its cuisine, and there is a traditional English-style pub offering draught beers and bar snacks ☎ 460-1058 Fax 460-1529.

$ EP Cortsland Hotel, Upper Gables, a delightful country inn set in tropical gardens and close to the airport and St John's ☎ 462-1395.

$$$ AI Curtain Bluff Resort, Old Road. This modern all-inclusive resort sits in lush tropical gardens at the end of the private Curtain Bluff peninsula which runs between two beautiful beaches ☎ 462-8400 Fax 462-8409.

$$ Dickenson Bay Cottages, offers one, two and three bedroom cottages on the hillside overlooking the bay and set in beautiful tropical gardens. It is a three minute walk to the ☎ 462-4940.

$$ EP Falmouth Harbour Beach Apartments, Falmouth Harbour. There are 20 fully equipped, self-catering studio apartments either on or close to the beach ☎ 460-1027 Fax 460-1534.

$$$ EP Hawksbill Beach Resort, Five Islands. Set in 37 acres (15 hectares) of lovely tropical gardens overlooking the sweeping bay and four exclusive beaches ☎ 462-0301 Fax 462-1515.

$-$$ EP Heritage Hotel, Heritage Quay St Mary's Street, St John's. Studio and one and two bedroom suites, ideal for business visitors. Facilities include meeting rooms, secretarial services with all amenities close by ☎ 462-1247 Fax 462-1179.

$$-$$$ EP Hodges Bay Club Resort, Hodges Bay, offers comfort, luxury and privacy. All villas have private balconies with sea views, and facilities include restaurant, bar, swimming pool, children's wading-pool, tennis and watersports ☎ 462-2300 Fax 462-1962.

$$$ EP The Inn at English Harbour, There are 6 hillside rooms and 22 beachfront rooms in the two story property in a corner of Freeman's Bay on ten acres (4 hectares) of national park beside the white sand beach and set among the palm trees ☎ 460-1014 Fax 460-1603.

$$ Jolly Harbour Beach Resort, Offers 20 self contained privately-owned beachfront villas, some with their own moorings ☎ 462-6166 Fax 462-6167.

$$ EP Jolly Harbour Marina Sports Centre and Golf Club, Lignumvitae Bay. Situated on a magnificent beach and in a complex covering 500 acres (200 hectares ☎ 462-3085 Fax 462-7686.

$$$ AI Mango Bay Hotel and Beach Club, a 64 room all-inclusive resort overlooking Dian Bay on the north east corner of the island. There is a thatched lagoon-side restaurant, three tier swimming pool and private beach ☎ 460-6646 Fax 460-8400.

$$-$$$ EP The New Barrymore Beach Club, Fort Road, is 2 miles (3km) from St John's and 7 miles (11km) from the airport, and set in tropical gardens alongside a fabulous white sand, palm-fringed beach ☎ 462-1055 Fax 462-4062.

$$$ AI Pineapple Beach Club, Long Bay. In a secluded setting along a lovely beach. The all-inclusive resort has 130 rooms with tennis, nightly live entertainment, physical fitness exercise equipment, walking trails, snorkeling, windsurfing and instruction. Wedding and honeymoon packages are available ☎ 463-2006.

$$ EP Rex Blue Heron Beach Hotel, Johnson's Point. This two-floor 64-room beachside property enjoys a sheltered position because

of the hills behind. The hotel has a terrace restaurant and bar, live entertainment most nights, and offers windsurfing, sailing, scuba, snorkeling, water-skiing and beautiful beaches ☎ 462-8564/6 Fax 462-8005.

$$$ EP/MAP Rex Halcyon Cove Beach Resort, Dickenson Bay. There are 210 luxury, spacious rooms and suites set in beautiful tropical flower gardens running down to the white sand beach and turquoise water Facilities include tennis with floodlit courts, freshwater swimming pool, free sailing, windsurfing, pedalos, snorkeling, water-skiing, scuba and deep sea fishing. There are also shops, boutiques, live entertainment, 2 restaurants – Warri Pier and The Terrace and 4 bars ☎ 460-0256 Fax 462-0271.

$$$ EP Royal Antiguan Beach and Tennis Resort, Deep Bay. A luxury high rise resort with 282 rooms and 12 one-bedroom garden and poolside cottages scattered through the extensive 150 acres (60 hectares) of lush, tropical gardens alongside a half mile (80m) long beach. Facilities include 3 restaurants, 5 bars, casino, boutiques, gym, hair salon, floodlit tennis, tennis pro shop, scuba and dive shop, pool, windsurfing, water-skiing, kayaks, sailing, entertainment, children's playground and shopping arcade. It has extensive conference and banqueting facilities and also offers honeymoon packages ☎ 462-3733 Fax 462-3732.

$$$ EP St James's Club, Mamora Bay. Occupies 100 acres (40 hectares) of a private peninsula jutting out into the mouth of the

Fact File

bay. There are 73 two-bedroom villas, 20 suites and 85 rooms all with bay or ocean view ☎ 460-5000 Fax 460-3015.

$$$ AI Sandals Antigua Resort, Dickenson Bay. A luxury all-inclusive coules-only resort set in 19 acres (7.6 hectares) of tropical, manicured gardens. It has 149 luxuriously decorated rooms, a choice of 3 restaurants and bars, live entertainment, disco, 5 swimming pools, jacuzzis, health spa, floodlit tennis, watersports and planned activities ☎ 462-0267.

$$ Sandpiper Reef Resort, a new 22-room and 2-suite resort 10 minutes from the airport and close to the Cedar Valley Golf Course ☎ 462-0939 Fax 462-1743.

$-$$ Sunsail Club Colonna, close to the airport this 100-room, apartment and villa property boasts the biggest pool on the island. There are two restaurants: a buffet style beach restaurant and The Coast – offering seafood and international dishes. There are three bars including the Sugar Mill Bar which provides gentle late night music and an American games room ☎ 462-6263 Fax 462-6430.

$$-$$$ EP Trafalgar Beach Villas, Pillar Rock Bay. Set in 5 acres (2 hectares) of gardens that run down to the secluded white sand beach ☎ 462-2531 Fax 462-2548.

REAL ESTATE, PROPERTY MANAGEMENT AND RENTAL SERVICES

Caribbean Properties, PO Box 1559, Falmouth, Antigua ☎ 462-1873

Tradewind Realty, Falmouth, Antigua ☎ 460-1082

Barbuda

Accommodation on the island is limited and in demand, so early reservations are strongly recommended.

$$$ The Coco Point Lodge
A discreet, exclusive, award-winning all-inclusive 34-room property on the beach which attracts the rich, the famous and the discerning, many of whom return year after year. It is set on a secluded 164-acre (66-hectare) peninsula close to the south-east tip of the island, and has been voted 'one of the most captivating resorts in the world' and described as 'simplicity with perfection.'

All the rooms, catering for a maximum of 68 guests, are in beachside bungalows and cottages, each with its own deck looking out over the Caribbean. The property, founded in 1960 by American entrepreneur William Cody Kelly and still owned by the Kelly family, is edged by 2.5 miles (4km) of white sand beach and surrounded by superb pristine beaches. It has its own lighted airstrip where guests arrive by private plane from Antigua's international airport. The resort is noted for its low-key luxury and comfort, qualities which bring back many of its guests year after year for the house party atmosphere created by Britons Caroline and Martin Price who have been resident managers since 1980. The tropical garden restaurant serves the finest local lobster, seafood and freshly baked bread and pastries, and is noted for its home-made soups and bisques. It also imports the best produce from around the world including French cheeses and fine wines.

The all-inclusive facilities include all-weather tennis, sunfish, sailing, windsurfing, water-skiing, sea-kayaking, snorkeling and equipment, deep sea fishing aboard the 43-foot (13m) motor yacht *Barbuda Belle*, reef and bone fishing with tackle provided, and informal trap shooting. Vehicles are also available with local guides for sightseeing ☎ 462-3816 Fax: 462-5340 (US ☎ 212-986-1416).

$$$ The K Club
The island's other exclusive, all-inclusive resort and owned by the world famous Milanese designer Krizia. It has 42 beautiful rooms set in 230 acres (92 hectares) of tropical gardens alongside a 3.5-mile (5.6km) white sand beach. 35 of the rooms are villas and cottages with mini-kitchens and private balconies. Guests include the rich and famous, and are met on arrival in Antigua and flown to Barbuda in the Club's private 8-seater plane. The property has a 9-hole golf course, the only one on Barbuda. Facilities also include tennis, snorkeling, windsurfing, sunfish and sailboats. Fishing and scuba diving trips can be arranged ☎ 460-0305.

$$ Earl's Villa and Efficiencies
This four-bedroom villa and self contained units are set in five acres (2 hectares) of land, one mile (1.6km) from Codrington Village and ten minutes drive to the nearest beach. Cook service and Jeep rental are available ☎ 462-5647.

VILLAS AND PRIVATE HOMES

Chrissy House
A 3-bedroom house in Codrington Village which offers use of a vehicle, baby sitting and cleaning.

AIRLINES/AIRPORTS

Air Canada	☎ 462-1147/800-422-6232
Air France	☎ 01159-082-6221
Air St Kitts-Nevis	☎ 465-8571
American Airlines	☎ 462-0950/800-433-7300
British Airways	☎ 462-0879/800-247-9297
BWIA	☎ 480-2925/462-1260
Carib Aviation	☎ 462-3147
Carib Express	☎ 462-0876
Caribbean Helicopters	☎ 460-5900
Condor/Lufthansa	☎ 462-0987/800-645-3880
Continental	☎ 462-5353/800-231-0856
LIAT	☎ 480-5600/5700
Norman Aviation	☎ 462-2445

BANKS

Most banks are open Monday to Thursday from 8am to 1pm, and on Friday from 8am to noon and 3pm to 5pm, although many may close for lunch. Some bank branches also open on Saturday morning from 8am to noon or 1pm.

Antigua Barbuda Investment Bank, High Street and Corn Alley, St John's ☎ 480-2700

Antigua Commercial Bank, St Mary's and Thames Street, St John's ☎ 462-1217

Bank of Antigua, High and Thames Streets, St John's ☎ 480-2700, Nelson's Dockyard ☎ 460-1367 and Airport Boulevard ☎ 463-5100

Bank of Nova Scotia, High Street, St John's ☎ 480-1500

Barclays Bank, High and Market Streets, St John's ☎ 480-5000

Caribbean Banking Corporation, High Street, St John's ☎ 462-4217

Royal Bank of Canada, High and Market Streets, St John's ☎ 480-1150

Swiss American Bank, Woods Estate, St John's ☎ 480-2240

Swiss-American National Bank of Antigua, High Street, St John's, ☎ 480-2230, and branches at Heritage Quay, Friar's Hill Road, Nelson'sDockyard, and Jolly Harbour

BEACHES/SWIMMING

There are fabulous beaches, everything you ever dreamed of for a tropical island, long stretches of sand, a fringe of tall palms for shade, and turquoise calm, clear warm seas. The beaches are clean, litter free and seldom crowded. The eastern beaches facing the Atlantic tend to have larger surf, while the western beaches offer more sheltered swimming.

Antigua boasts 365 white sand beaches – one for every day of the year, and Barbuda has miles of beautiful beaches. The longest beach runs for 7 miles (11km) and at certain times the sand turns pink because of millions of tiny particles of crushed coral and shell that are washed ashore.

All the beaches on the islands are public. The only officially designated nude beach is a remote area on Five Islands beyond the Hawksbill Beach Resort.

Best beaches on Antigua include:

Carlisle Bay	Fort James Bay	Lignumviatae Bay
Darkwood	Galley Bay	Long Bay
Deep Bay	Half Moon Bay	Mamora Bay
Dickenson Bay	Hawksbill Bay	Rendezvous Bay
Doigs Beach	Johnsons Bay	Runaway Bay…
Ffryes Bay	Jolly Beach	

and most of the other 350 beaches as well!

CAMPING

There are no official campsites on the islands.

CAR RENTAL/DRIVING

Cars, jeeps and other four-wheel-drive vehicles can be rented and provide the best way of exploring the islands. If you plan to go at peak periods it is best to rent your vehicle in advance through your travel agent. Cars can be rented, however, at airports, hotels or car rental offices on the island.

Car rental rates vary enormously but start from around US$40-50 a day for compact automatics, and from $50-60 for jeeps or other four-wheel-drive vehicles during the summer low season. Winter rates are higher, usually a little more expensive. There is quite a wide range of vehicles available and rates depend both on the type of vehicle and the rental company. There are usually quite a lot of incentives, so it pays to shop around.

To rent a car you must have a valid driving license which entitles you to receive a temporary 90 day local driving permit for a fee of EC$50 (US$20). You can get this at the airport or any police station, although most car rental companies now do this for you. An imprint of your credit card, which acts as a deposit, is usually required.

Before accepting the vehicle check it for scratches, dents and other problems, such as missing wing mirrors, and make sure these are clearly listed. Also check there is a spare wheel in good condition and a working jack. While there are several service stations around the island it is a good idea always to keep your fuel tank topped up.

DRIVE ON THE LEFT, stick to the speed limits and use a good map.

Driving under the influence of alcohol or drugs is against the law, and there are heavy penalties if convicted, especially as a result of an accident.

Avoid clearly marked 'no parking' zones or you might pick up a ticket, but parking generally does not pose a problem.

If you have an accident or breakdown during the day call your car rental company, so make sure you have the telephone number with you. They will usually send out a mechanic or a replacement vehicle. If you are stuck at night make sure the car is off the road, lock the vehicle and call a taxi to take you back to your hotel. Report the problem to the car rental company or the police as soon as possible.

Car and Scooter Rental companies

Anjam, Sunset Cove, Dickenson Bay ☎ 462-3765

Avis Rent A Car, VC Bird International Airport ☎ 462-AVIS/2840, St James's Club ☎ 462-5000

Bike Plus, Camacho's Avenue, ☎462-2453

Budget, VC Bird International Airport or free delivery and pick-up anywhere on the island ☎ 462-3009/3051/3056

Capital Rental and Tours, High Street, St John's, airport and hotel pick-up and delivery ☎ 460-7224

Carib Car Rentals, Hodges Bay, pick-up and delivery service ☎ 462-2062

Charles Car Rentals, Upper Gambies ☎ 462-4452

Dion's, at VC Bird International Airport ☎ 462-DION

Dollar, St John's and airport ☎ 462-0362

Hertz, All Saints Road, St Johns ☎ 462-4114, Jolly Harbour ☎ 462-6268, Dockyard Office ☎ 460-2617, and at the VC Bird International Airport

J&L, Crosbies ☎ 462-3285

Jonas Rent A Car, free pick-up from the airport and hotels ☎ 462-3760

Lion's Car Rental, English Harbour ☎ 460-1400

National Car Rental, All Saints Road, St Johns ☎ 462-0576

Prince's Rent A Car, Fort Road ☎ 462-0766

Richard's Car Rental, VC Bird International Airport ☎ 462-0976

Shipwreck Rent-A-Scooter Bicycles, English Harbour ☎ 4606087, St John's ☎ 464-7771

St John's Car Rental, St John's ☎ 462-0594

Sun Cycles, Nelson Drive, Ghodge's Bay ☎ 461-0324

Thrifty, VC Bird International Airport and island-wide delivery service ☎ 462-9523

Yati Scooters Rental, ☎ 462-7955

CASINOS

King's Casino, Heritage Quay, St John's	☎ 462-1727
Joe Mike's Downtown Hotel Plaza, St John's	☎ 462-9877
Keno Palaca Casino, St Mary's Street, St John's	☎ 462-9877
Speedy Joe's, Nevis Street, St John's	☎ 462-1141

CHURCHES

There are more than 100 churches on the island. Most of the people are Protestant, although many other faiths are represented including: Baha'i, Baptist, Church of Christ, Church of God, Jehovah's Witness, Methodist, Moravian, Pentecostal, Rastafarian, Roman Catholic and Seventh-Day Adventists.

CLOTHING

Casual is the keyword but you can generally be as smart or as cool as you like. There are a number of up-market restaurants and clubs where there are dress codes, and if you plan to visit these, you should pack accordingly. Beachwear is fine for the beach and pool areas, but cover up a little for the street. Informal is the order of the day and night, and this is not the place for suits and ties or evening gowns, unless you really like dressing up for dinner. During the day light, cotton, casual clothes are ideal for exploring in. During the evening a light jumper or wrap may sometimes be needed. It is fun to change for dinner but for men this normally means smart slacks or trousers, and for women a summer dress or similar. There are establishments, however, where sports coats or jackets are not out of place, and women can be as elegant as they wish.

If you plan to explore on foot, stout footwear and a good waterproof jacket are essential. Also, wear sunglasses and a hat to protect you from the sun during the hottest part of the day, and you will need sandals on the beach as the sand can get too hot to walk on in bare feet.

CURRENCY

The official currency on the islands is the East Caribbean dollar (EC$) which is fixed to the US dollar at about EC$2.6 to US$1.The EC$ rate against sterling fluctuates, but a general rule of thumb is to work on EC$4=£1. US dollars are widely accepted, as are all major credit cards. Currency can be exchanged at banks at fixed exchange rates, and at many hotels and stores, although the rate may not be as advantageous.

The American Express Card is the official card of the island, and their representative is Antours, Long and Thames Streets, St John's ☎ 462-4788.

Note: Always have a few small denomination notes for tips.

DEPARTURE TAX

There is a EC$50/US$20 departure tax payable at the airport check-in.

DISABLED FACILITIES

Many of the watersports and dive operations will accommodate disabled visitors. There are some facilities for the disabled at most of the larger resorts.

DRUGS

There are strict laws prohibiting the possession and use of drugs, including marijuana. Heavy fines and prison await those who ignore the law.

ELECTRICITY

The usual electricity supply is either 110 volts or 220 AC, 60 cycles, the former being the more common and suitable for US appliances. Most hotels have dual voltages. Adapters are necessary for European appliances without dual voltages, and may be available from your hotel.

EMBASSIES AND CONSULATES

British High Commission, Old Road, St John's   ☎ 462-0008
Chinese Embassy, Heritage Hotel, Antigua   ☎ 462-1125
Danish Consulate, High Street, St John's   ☎ 462-0183
Dutch Consulate, High Street, St John's   ☎ 462-0308
German Consulate, Hodges Bay, St John's   ☎ 462-3174/2824
Italian Consulate, Galleon Beach, Antigua   ☎ 460-1915
Norwegian Consulate, High Street, St John's   ☎ 462-0858
US Consular Office, St John's   ☎ 463-6531
Venezuelan Embassy, St John's   ☎ 462-1574

ESSENTIAL THINGS TO PACK

Sun block cream, sunglasses, sun hat, camera (and lots of film), insect repellent, binoculars if interested in bird watching and wildlife, and a small torch in case of power failures.

FESTIVALS/PUBLIC HOLIDAYS *

January
New Year's Day *
Annual Tennis Championships

February
Ash Wednesday (date varies)

March/April
Good Friday *(date varies)
Easter Monday *(date varies)
International Sailing Week
(runs into May)

May
Labour Day (first Monday)
Whit Monday
International Sailing Week
Lord Nelson's Ball
Annual Tennis Championships

July
Caricom Day (first Monday) *
Mid-summer Carnival (runs into August)

August
Mid-summer Carnival * (first Monday and Tuesday in August are the final days of Carnival)

November
Independence Day – 1 November *

December
Annual Tennis Championships
25th Christmas Day *
26th Boxing Day *
New Year's Eve

HEALTH

There are no serious health problems although visitors should take precautions against the sun, which can ruin your holiday. Injections are not required unless visiting from an infected area. All hotels have doctors either resident or on call, and standards of health care are generally high. There are two hospitals on Antigua, one public and a private clinic, and a small hospital on Barbuda.

Hospitals

Antigua
Holberton Hospital, Queen Elizabeth Highway ☎ 462-0251 (main hospital)

Gambles Medical Centre, Friars Hill Road and Mahoganey Drive ☎ 462-3050 (private clinic).

Barbuda
Spring View Hospital, ☎ 460-0409.

While there are several pharmacies, medication can be expensive and, if you are taking medicines on prescription, it is advisable to bring enough for your stay.

Tanning safely

The sun is very strong but sea breezes often disguise just how hot it is. If you are not used to the sun take it carefully for the first two or three days, use a good sun screen with a factor of 15 or higher, and do not sunbathe during the hottest parts of the day. Wear sunglasses and a sun hat. Sunglasses will protect you against the glare, especially strong on the beach, and sun hats will protect your head.

If you spend a lot of time swimming or scuba diving take extra care as you will burn even quicker because of the combination of salt water and sun.

Calamine lotion and preparations containing aloe are both useful in combating sunburn.

Irritating insects

Mosquitoes are not much of a problem on or near the beaches because of onshore winds, but they may well bite you as you enjoy an open air evening meal. Use a good insect repellent, particularly if you are planning trips inland.

Lemon grass can sometimes be found growing naturally, and a handful of this in your room is also a useful mosquito deterrent.

Sand-flies can be a problem on the beach. Despite their tiny size they can give you a nasty bite. And ants exist, so make sure you check the ground carefully before sitting down otherwise you might get bitten, and the bites can itch for days.

Note: Drinking water from the tap in hotels and resorts is generally safe although bottled mineral and distilled water are widely available.

LANGUAGE

The official language spoken is English.

LOST PROPERTY

Report lost property as soon as possible to your hotel or the nearest police station.

NIGHTLIFE/NIGHTCLUBS

There is a great choice of entertainment from superb dining to cabaret, and karaoke bars to casinos. Many of the larger hotels and resorts offer live entertainment such as steel bands, combos and dancers, and there are bars, dancing and discos, mostly in and around St John's and English Harbour. You can hear great jazz all over Antigua. And, for something really exciting, experience a night dive. Don't miss the Shirley Heights Jump-up.

There are several discos and night spots in St John's and English Harbour. **King's Casino**, Heritage Quay, St John's (☎ 462-1727) offers gambling. **The Lemon Tree** in St John's (☎ 462-1969) has great live entertainment and dancing, as does **Ribbit**, Green Bay (☎ 462-7996), **Safari Club**, **Tradewinds** (☎ 463-8003) and **Shirley Heights Lookout** (☎ 460-1785), the latter being a great place to spend Sunday afternoon and evening.

Also check out:

Miller's By The Sea, live music – from jazz to calypso – every night.

Shooters, Tradewinds. Lively theme night bar offering disco, jazz, games and partying. Open daily except Tuesday from 8pm to late ☎ 462-1501.

Windies, Redcliffe Quay, St John's. Open Friday and Saturday from 10pm until late. Admission charge.

Other Nightclubs

Cats, Sunset Cover, Runaway Bay	☎ 462-3762
Jackpot Casino, High Street, St John's	☎ 462-2359

PERSONAL INSURANCE AND MEDICAL COVER

Make sure you have adequate personal insurance and medical cover. If you need to call out a doctor or have medical treatment, you will probably have to pay for it at the time, so keep all receipts so that you can reclaim on your insurance.

PHARMACIES

Alpha Pharmacy, Redcliffe Street, St John's	☎ 462-1112
Benjies Pharmacy, Redcliffe Street, St John's	☎ 462-0733
City Pharmacy, St Mary's Street, St John's	☎ 462-1363
Gore's Drug Store, Market Street, St John's	☎ 462-1153
Harbour Pharmacy, Jolly Harbour	☎ 462-6069
Joseph's Pharmacy, Redcliffe Street, St John's	☎ 462-1025

Piper's Pharmacy, All Saints Road, St John's ☎ 462-0736
Reliance Pharmacy, Redcliffe Street, St John's ☎ 462-4646
Shopper's Drug Store, High and Temple
  Streets, St John's ☎ 462-4706

PHOTOGRAPHY

The intensity of the sun can play havoc with your films, especially if photographing near water or white sand.

Compensate for the brightness otherwise your photographs will come out over exposed and wishy-washy.

The heat can actually damage film so store reels in a box or bag in the hotel fridge if there is one.

Also remember to protect your camera if on the beach, as a single grain of sand is all it takes to jam the mechanism.

It is very easy to get 'click happy' so be tactful and polite when taking photographs. Many islanders are shy or simply fed up with being photographed. You will have to decide whether the picture is worth it, but if a person declines to have their photograph taken, don't ignore this. The islanders are a warm and very hospitable people and if you stop and spend some time finding out what they are doing they will usually then allow you to take a photograph.

POLICE

Police Headquarters is on American Road on the outskirts of St John's and there is a police station on the corner of Newgate and Market Streets.

PORTS

The main port is St John's although English Harbour is the home of the island's charter fleet.

POST OFFICE

The Post Office is in Long Street just north of Heritage Quay, St John's. Open Monday to Thursday from 8.15am to 12 noon and from 1pm to 4pm (5pm Friday) ☎ 462-0023.
The Lady Hamilton, Upper Redcliffe Street, St John's, is the only stamp shop on the island for philatelists.

PUBLIC TOILETS

There are not many public toilets on the island, but bars, restaurants and hotels have private facilities which can usually be used if you ask politely.

RESTAURANTS (SEE PAGES 64-67)

There is a remarkably large choice when it comes to eating out on the island. There are the inevitable fast food burger, pizza and fried chicken outlets, beach cafés offering excellent value for money, and elegant up-market dining rooms, as well as restaurants offering a wide range of ethnic cuisine's, from Caribbean cooking to Chinese.

Most accept credit cards and during peak times of the year reservations are recommended. If you come across a restaurant not listed in the guide, or have comments about any of those that are, I would very much like to hear from you. Write to me c/o Gulf Atlantic Publishing, 1947 Lee Road, Winter Park, FL 32789 USA.

Some restaurants are closed on Saturday for lunch and all day Sunday, but hotel restaurants are open daily and welcome outside guests. The restaurants listed in the itineraries are classified by price – $ inexpensive, $$ moderate, $$$ expensive. See end of chapter 2 for restaurant listings.

SECURITY

There is little serious crime but as anywhere it makes sense not to walk around wearing expensive jewels or flashing large sums of money. Secure your valuables as you should anywhere, and do not leave items unattended on the beach or in an unlocked car.

Don't carry around your passport or all your money. Keep them secure in your room or in a hotel safety deposit box. It is also a good idea to have photocopies of the information page of your passport, your air ticket and holiday insurance policy. All will help greatly if the originals are lost.

SERVICE CHARGES AND TAXES

There is a government tax of 8.5 per cent on accommodation and restaurant bills. A 10-15 per cent service charge may also be added to restaurant bills. Menus and tariffs sometimes include these charges so check to make sure they have not been added again. In shops the price on the label is what you pay.

SHELLS

Shells are washed up on to the beaches but they should be left for others to enjoy. Live shells may not be taken by collectors.

SHOPPING

Antigua has excellent duty-free shopping from top name designer clothes, to fine china and crystal, perfumes and jewels, and island goods such as handprints, paintings, and spices. Shops are generally open from 8am to 4 or 4.30pm Monday to Friday and on Saturday from 8am to noon. Some still close for lunch between noon and 1.30pm and many in St John's close at noon on Thursday. The main shopping areas are in St John's, the two most fashionable areas being Heritage Quay and Redcliffe Quay, and both open on Sunday if a cruise ship is in port. It is also worth exploring the many streets inland from the waterfront for their interesting and varied shops. There is also good shopping at Jolly Harbour, and many of the hotels and resorts have their own boutiques and shops.

Best buys include: local hand-crafted goods such as straw weaving, pottery, batik, silk-screened printed fabrics, wood carvings and paintings, and Antigua rum. Duty-free bargains include rings, necklaces, etc, watches, perfumes, crystal, china, fine linen and designer sports clothing and beachwear.

Apart from the specialist shops mentioned under Heritage Quay and Recliffe Quay on pages 38/39, the following are among those offering island arts and crafts:

Arty Crafts, Halcyon Cove Hotel
Harmony Hall, Freetown
Industrial Workshop for the Blind, All Saints Road
The Restoration Gift Shop, Nelson's Dockyard
Shirley Heights Lookout Gift Shop
Susie's Hot Sauce, Upper North Street, St John's

SIGHTSEEING AND TOURS

Sightseeing and island tours by land or sea can be arranged through hotels, tour representatives or one of the many specialist tour companies on the island. These include:

Alexander Parrish, Thames Street, St John's. Travel service, tours, transfers, bilingual guides ☎ 462-0638.

Antours, Long and Thames Streets, St Johns. Tours and transfers, multilingual representatives ☎ 462-4788.

Caribbean Helicopters, Global Travel and Tours, High Street, St John's ☎ 462-4784, and Falmouth ☎ 460-3354.

Caribrep, wide range of tours, including day trips to Barbuda taking in lunch and visits to all the sights ☎ 462-0818.

Global Travel and Tours, High Street, St John's ☎ 480-1230.

JetSet International Travel Agency, Nelson's Dockyards, tours and day charters ☎ 460-1721.

Kiskidee ☎ 462-4801

Tropikelly Trails, four-wheel-drive, off-road adventure tours ☎ 461-0383.

SPORT

Cricket is the national game and played with such a vehemence that it is not surprising that the West Indies are world champions. Island cricket stars include Andy Roberts, Richie Richardson, the former West Indies captain, and the legendary Viv Richards, one of the greatest cricketers of all times.

The game is played at every opportunity and anywhere. You can be driving in the countryside, turn a corner and confront players using the road as a wicket. It is played on the beach using a strip of palm for a bat, and even in the water if the tide is coming in. If the island team or the West Indies is playing, almost all the radios on the island are tuned in for the commentary, and matches always draw capacity crowds with a festive atmosphere and picnics. The cricket season lasts from January to May with matches played between island teams, inter-island sides and international test teams.

For the visitor there is a huge range of sporting opportunities from swimming and scuba diving, to hiking and tennis or having a game of cricket with one of the local teams. There is cycling, sailing, squash and, of course, fishing either from shore or boat. The north and east coasts offer stronger swells for windsurfing and surfing but the seas can sometimes be rough and care is needed, while the west and south coast beaches offer safe swimming.

Most hotels offer a variety of sports and water activities, and dive operators offer all levels of instruction. You can learn what it is all about and progress to advanced level if you have the time.

Walking is great fun and there are lots of trails but have stout, non-slip footwear and take a waterproof. Protect yourself against insects, carry adequate drinking water and keep an eye on the time, because night falls quickly and you don't want to be caught out on the trail after dark.

Cycling

Bikes are a good way of getting around and getting a tan. **Sun Cycles** offers short and long-term rentals with free pick-up and delivery ☎ 461-0324.

Fitness Gyms

Many of the main hotels and resorts offer health and fitness facilities. In addition there are:

BBR Sportive, Jolly Harbour with squash floodlit tennis and 82-foot (25m) pool. It is open daily from 8am to 9pm and food and soft drinks are available ☎ 462-6260.

Fitness Shak, Dickenson Bay, full gym ☎ 462-5223.

Lotus Health Center, Dickenson Bay, offers massage, herbal facial, acupuncture and foot reflexology. It is open Monday to Saturday from 10am to 6pm ☎ 462-2231.

National Fitness Center, a ten-minute walk from the middle of St John's (just to warm you up), with weight and fitness training equipment, step and aerobic classes. Open Monday to Friday from 6am to 10am and noon to 8pm, and on Saturday from 9am to 2pm ☎ 462-3681.

Qua Sha Health Center, Hudson Street, St John's, offers Chinese therapy, including massage, acupuncture, reflexology and herbal weight loss.
For appointments ☎ 461-6777.

St James Club, Mamora Bay, hairdresser, massage and beauty treatments ☎ 460-5000.

Temo Sports, English Harbour has floodlit tennis plus squash courts and equipment can be rented. There is also a bar and bistro. It is open Monday to Saturday from 7am to 10pm ☎ 460-1781.

Therapeutic and Sports Massage, St John's ☎ 463-4346.

Tree House, English Harbour, complete body shop for men and women ☎ 460-3434.

Fishing

Fishing is an island pursuit, and many islanders will fish for hours from quayside walls, from the beach or river side.

There is year-round world-class deep sea and game fishing for Atlantic blue marlin, skipjack, blackfin and yellowfin tuna also called allison, which can weigh over 100lbs (45.5kg), wahoo and white marlin which can weigh more than 100lbs (45.5kg), and the fighting sailfish. Snapper, bonefish, permit, pompano, tarpon, grouper, bonito and barracuda can all be caught close to shore. Around the reefs there is an abundance of grouper, jack crevalle, mutton snapper and yellowtail snapper. Dorado is usually called dolphin (not the mammal but the fish also known as mahi-mahi).

There are many guides and charter boats for rent. Prices vary enormously depending on the vessel, number of lines allowed and facilities offered. Fishing charters are offered by :

Jacal	☎ 461-2368	*Nimrod*	☎ 464-0143
Legend	☎ 462-0256	*Obsession*	☎ 462-3174
Lobster King	☎ 462-4363	*Overdraft*	☎ 462-0649
Misa Ferdie	☎ 462-1440	*Shadowhawk*	☎ 462-0256
Miss Ashley	☎ 462-9717	*Tito I*	☎ 460-1452

(see under Yachting and boating for further details)

Golf

There are three golf courses – Cedar Valley, Half Moon Bay and Jolly Harbour on Antigua. **Cedar Valley** is a 6,100-yard (5.6km) , 71-par, 18-hole championship course which hosts the annual Antiguan Open tournament each March. There is a pro shop, snack shop and bar ☎ 462-0161.

Half Moon Bay is a spectacular 34-par, 9-hole course where it is easy to be distracted from your game by the magnificent views of the beach and sea ☎ 460-4300.

The newest 6,000 yard (5.5km) 71-par 18-hole Harbour Club course is at **Jolly Harbour**. There is a pro shop and club house ☎ 463-8830. All the courses are open to the public and clubs can be rented.

Barbuda offers the 9-hole course at the **K-Club** ☎ 460-0275.

Hiking

There are some spectacular walks around the coast and inland both on Antigua and Barbuda. It is essential to drink plenty of water and take frequent rests, as the walking may be more tiring than you think, and wear sensible, sturdy footwear.

Horseback Racing and Riding

There are several stables on the island and horseback riding can be arranged through hotels. **Spring Hill Riding Club** is on the road to Rendezvous Bay, and offers instruction from BHS qualified staff. There is a floodlit course, cross-country course and range of ponies and horses to suit all sizes and levels of experience. Full and half-day trips can be arranged taking in beach rides, national parks and forest landscapes. Open from 7.30am Tuesday to Sunday for morning sessions, and from 3.30pm for afternoon rides ☎ 460-1333/2700.

Horse racing takes place at Cassada Gardens, north east of St John's and near the airport, on most public holidays.

Hunting

There is seasonal deer hunting on Barbuda. A license is required and can be obtained from the police station in Codrington Village.

Scuba diving

The waters offer some of the best diving in the world and are warm (average temperatures being 80°F, 25°C) and remarkably clear with excellent visibility ranging from 50 to 140 feet (15-43m). The fringe barrier reefs are easily accessible and they teem with different corals and marine life – there are almost 400 species of fish. Many of the reefs and shipwrecks are close to the shore, while there are walls, drop-offs, caves and tunnels to explore in deeper waters. Off the south coast of Antigua fallen rocks have created an area of caves and gulleys which is fascinating to explore. The east coast of Antigua offers good diving for experienced divers but the sea conditions can change quickly, and you should only dive with an experienced dive master.

Barbuda is surrounded by reefs and many wrecks, although large areas are still unexplored.

The best Antigua dive sites listed by the tourist office include:

SOUTH-WEST COAST

Cades Reef is an extensive formation stretching for 2 miles (3km) with rich fish life and a wide variety of soft and hard coral. Visibility is generally excellent and waters are smooth. Ideal for both scuba and snorkeling.

The Chimney features a small cave at a depth of 60 feet (18m) with sponge-filled gullies as deep as 80 feet (24m). The Chimney is home to many different species of fish including large parrot fish, eels, lobsters and harmless nurse sharks.

Monk's Head gets its name from the coral formations which have sand in the middle and look like a monk's tonsure. Large stingrays swim in the area and you may spot one of the rare eels that inhabit the reef.

Ariadne Shoal is a long ride, taking almost an hour from most dive shops, but well worth the effort. You can dive down to the reefs at a depth of 50-80 feet (15-24m) where there are large fish and lobsters, turtles and nurse sharks.

WEST COAST

The Knoll is a beautiful coral head 'forest' at a depth of 50 feet (15m) covered in sea fans and soft coral rising to within 25 feet (7m) of the surface.

Thunderhead is a wreck-strewn reef in shallow waters only a short boat ride out. Most of the reef is in 35 feet (11m) of water although it slopes away gently and you can explore the hard coral and search for treasure.

The Ridge is a wall dive dropping from 25 feet (7m) to the sea bed at 60 feet (18m). The wall is covered in small coral heads which are home to thousands of small fish. Nurse sharks swim in the area and you may see an occasional turtle.

The **Andes** is the wreck of a merchant ship which sank in 1905 and now lies in 20 feet (6m) of water at the mouth of Deep Bay. It is now overgrown with coral and home to thousands of brightly hued fish, including the occasional puffer fish.

NORTH AND NORTH-WEST COASTS

Jettias is a dive site over the 310 feet (95m) freighter which sank in 1917 and now lies in just 25 feet (7m) of water, which makes it an easy dive even for inexperienced divers and underwater photography.

Stingray Bank is appropriately named, and one of the best dive sites around the island when the sea conditions are right and the waters are calm. This is another excellent site for underwater photographers.

SOUTH COAST

Shirley Heights has many dive sites inshore as the waters drop to a depth of 100 feet (30m). There are coral ledges, walls and drop-offs, and interesting rock formations that are the homes of rays and spade fish and also shelter the occasional turtle.

Sunken Rock is for experienced divers only and begins at a depth of about 40 feet (12m) where there is a coral encrusted canyon. This can be followed to a sandy ledge, from where the rock face drops quickly to well below 120 feet (37m). Here you can dive among the barracuda, rays and amberjack.

DIVE COMPANIES AND DIVE SCHOOLS

Aquanaut Diving Center, St James's Club, Marmora Bay, offers PADI, NAUI and NASE certification courses ☎ 462-1430

Big John's Dive Antigua, Dickenson Bay, offers NAUI courses ☎ 462-3483

Deep Bay Divers, Redcliffe Quay, St John's ☎ 463-8000

Dive Runaway, Runaway Bay, is a full PADI dive facility offering courses from beginner to assistant instructor ☎ 462-2626

Dockyard Divers, English Harbour ☎ 460-1178

Jolly Dive, Jolly Harbour ☎ 462-8305

Long Bay Dive Shop, Long Bay ☎ 463-2005

Pirate Divers, Dutchman's Bay ☎ 462-3094

The following hotels offer dive packages:

Curtain Bluff ☎ 462-8400

Jumby Bay ☎ 462-6000

Fact File

Snorkeling

Many reefs lie close to the shore and are easily accessible. Glass-bottom boats and other charter vessels go to deeper reefs where you can snorkel. The following offer snorkeling trips:

Jacal	☎ 462-2650	*Miguel's Holiday*	
Kokomo Cat	☎ 462-7245	*Adventure*	☎ 461-0361
Loafer	☎ 462-2690	*Nimrod*	☎ 464-0143
Lobster King	☎ 462-4363	*Sentio*	☎ 464-7127
		Tito I	☎ 460-1452

Squash

There are facilities at **BBR Sportive** at Jolly Harbour ☎ 462-6260 and **Temo Sports** in English Harbour ☎ 460-1781.

Tennis

The Annual Tennis Championships are held in January, May and December and attract top ranking US and European players.

There are many courts on all the islands, some floodlit, and many hotels offer tennis packages which include court time and coaching. Some of the larger hotels also host annual tennis tournaments. Not all hotel courts are open to the public.

If newly arrived on the island, book a court early in the morning or late in the afternoon when it is cooler until you get used to the heat.

WATERSPORTS AND AQUATIC ACTIVITIES

These are available at all resorts and most large hotels and range from Hobie Cats, jet skis, windsurfers, kayaks and sunfish. Experts are also on hand to teach you how to sail, water-ski and parasail. Water-skiers must always operate well away from swimmers. There is excellent windsurfing on Antigua and Barbuda because of the year round onshore trade winds. There are beginners' schools on the more sheltered west coast, while intermediate and experienced windsurfers can enjoy the Atlantic rollers on the east coast. Galley Bay and Turtle Bay offer the best year-round surfing.

Halcyon Cove Watersports, water-skiing and small boats for rent ☎ 462-0256.

Offshore Sport, rents pleasure boats for exploring the coastline. Boats can be picked up at Heritage or Redcliffe Quays in St John's. Open daily from 8.30am to 4.30pm ☎ 462-4886.

Patrick's Windsurfing School, expert tuition for beginners at the Halcyon Cove Hotel, and intermediate and advanced courses at the Lord Nelson Beach Club at Dutchman's Bay ☎ 462-3094/0256.

Runaway Sport, Runaway Bat, water-skiing, windsurfing, jet bikes, banana rides and canoes ☎ 462-3281.

Wadaldi Windsurfers, Lord Nelson Hotel ☎ 462-2980.

Windsurfing Antigua, Dutchman's and Dickenson Bay ☎ 462-9463.

YACHTING AND BOATING, MARINAS AND BERTHING FACILITIES

The offshore waters are a Mecca for yachtsmen from around the world. English Harbour is the main base for the island's famous yacht charter fleet.

International Sailing Week takes place at the end of April and beginning of May. It is the premiere regatta in the Caribbean and one of the top five in the world. The annual regatta attracts entries from throughout the Caribbean, Europe, and North and South America. Apart from the yacht races, this is the time for great beach parties and meeting people, culminating in the award ceremony at the Lord Nelson's Ball held at the Admiral's Inn, English Harbour.

Yacht charters

Nicholson's Yacht Charters	☎ 1-800-662-6066
Sun Yacht Charters, Nelson's Dockyard	☎ 469-2115

Marinas

Antigu Slipway, Nelson's Dockyard, English Harbour	☎ 460-1056
Antigua Yacht Club and Marina, Falmouth Harbour	☎ 460-1879
Catamaran Hotel and Marina, Falmouth Harbour	☎ 460-1036
Crabbs Slipway and Marina	☎ 463-3750
Jolly Harbour Marino, Jolly Harbour	☎ 462-6041
St James's Yacht Club, Mamora Bay	☎ 460-5000
Redcliffe Quay Marina, St John's	☎ 462-1847

Cruises and water sightseeing trips

There are tours aboard glass-bottomed boats to the many nature islands off Antigua, and these offer an excellent way of viewing the rich marine life and coral reefs.

Horatio Historic Cruises, operates 30 minute cruises around Nelson's Dockyard. They run daily every 30 minutes from 10am to 5pm ☎ 460-1178.

Jacal, a 25-foot (8m) Mako, runs fishing, snorkeling and picnic cruises. They even offer golfing trips across to Montserrat and Nevis ☎ 462-26050.

Jolly Roger Pirate Cruises, fun cruises daily with wining, dining and dancing, swimming and snorkeling ☎ 462-2064.

Kokomo Cat Cruises, a 61-foot (18m) catamaran – *Kokomo* – sails to nearby islands and secluded beaches for snorkeling and picnics, as well as running sunset cruises ☎ 462-7245.

Lamarine, Jolly Harbour, a variety of boats for rent ☎ 462-7686.

Legend, a 35-foot (11m) Hatteras sport fishing boat available for fishing trips and cruises ☎ 462-0256.

Loafer, a magnificent 70-foot (21m) catamaran which offers sailing, sightseeing and snorkeling trips ☎ 462-2690.

Lobster King, offers half and full day fishing charters, plus trips to the nearby islands of Montserrat, St Martin, Dominica and Barbuda aboard the 38-foot (12m) *Bertram*. The Lobster King Glass Bottom Boat offers daily three-hour cruises with snorkeling, music and open bar, plus the Friday lobster picnic cruise ☎ 462-4363.

Miguel's Holiday Adventure sails from Hodges Bay on Tuesday, Thursday and Saturday at 10am for the five-minute crossing to Prickly Pear Island, where the day can be spent on the beach fishing, swimming, snorkeling and picnicking. All equipment is included. The boat returns at 4pm. Special trips can be arranged ☎ 461-0361.

M/Y Nimrod, a 50-foot (15m) professionally crewed sport fishing boat fully equipped for deep sea fishing charters, scuba and snorkeling. It is based in Falmouth Harbour ☎ 464-0143.

Obsession, a 45-foot (14m) Hatteras sport fishing boat equipped to the highest specifications, and offering deep sea fishing and sightseeing trips. It sails from the Falmouth Harbour marina ☎ 462-3174.

Off Wind offers full day or overnight cruises ☎ 460-9210.

Paradise I, a French-built 45-foot (14m) sailing yacht that can accommodate up to 14 people.

It offers full day sailing cruises including lunch and open bar, and is also available for charter ☎ 462-4158.

Quick Getaway, an elegant 40-foot (12m) sloop offering half and full day cruises and available for charter ☎ 462-0256.

Sagitoo Catamaran Cruise offers round the island, sunset, moonlight and archaeological cruises, as well as day trips to Barbuda and Montserrat ☎ 460-1244.

Sea Sports, Dickenson Bay ☎ 462-3355

Sentio, a 45-foot (14m) luxury sailing ketch which is ideal for small groups, honeymooners and special occasions. It sails to secluded beaches for picnics and snorkeling, and also offers half and full day cruises, learn-to-sail cruises, sunset and overnight trips to Barbuda ☎ 464-7127.

Shorty's Glass Bottom Boat offers two cruises daily from Dickenson Bay to the offshore reefs.

Tito I, is a powerful 34-foot (10m) Scarab Supersport with twin engines, offering day tours to nearby islands and remote beaches for swimming, picnicking and snorkeling. Deep sea fishing charters are also available ☎ 460-3336.

Treasure Island Cruises, cruise to the music of a steel band with full buffet, open bar, limbo and lots of fun ☎ 461-8698.

Wadaldi Cats, Redcliffe Quay, St John's ☎ 462-4792

TAXIS

Antigua Taxi Stand, Market Street	☎ 462-0711
Brothers, Lower Long Street, St John's	☎ 462-6464
Christo, High Street, St John's	☎ 460-7434
Heritage Quay Taxi Stand, St John's	☎ 460-8213
Ivor's Taxi, Liberta Village	☎ 460-1241
Reliable Taxi Service, Clark's Hill	☎ 462-1510
Sandals Antigua Taxi Stand	☎ 462-2504
Twenty Four Hours Taxi Service	☎ 462-5190
West Bus Station Taxis, St John's	☎ 462-5190

TELEPHONES

International communications on the island are provided by Cable and Wireless, whose main office is in St Mary's Street, St John's ☎ 462-0840. There is also a sub office in Nelson's Dockyard ☎ 460-1479.

The international code for Antigua is 268. From the US dial 1-268 and the seven-digit island number. Direct calling is available to and from most countries. From the UK and Europe dial 001-268 and the seven-digit island number. To ring the US from Antigua dial 1 + area code + seven-digit local number. To use AT&T Direct dial 1-800-872-2881 or #1. To ring the UK from Antigua dial 011-44-area code+seven-digit local number. For credit card calls dial 1-800-877-8000. Cellular phones can be rented through Boatphone ☎ 462-5051, if you want to stay in touch or are planning to cruise for a few days. Many establishments can also be contacted by radio phone on one of the VHF Channels.

TIME

Antigua operates under Eastern Standard Time Zone, and Eastern Daylight Time between April and October. During the winter Antigua is four hours behind London and during the summer five hours.

TIPPING

Tips are generally added to restaurant bills but check in case they are not, in which case add 10-15 per cent. It is customary to tip bellboys in hotels, taxi drivers, guides and other people providing a service. Tip taxi drivers around 10-15 per cent and bellboys $1 for each piece of luggage.

TOURIST OFFICES

The **Antigua and Barbuda Tourist Office** is at:
Thames and High Streets, PO Box 363, St John's, Antigua
☎ 268-462-0480 Fax 268-2483. There are Tourist Information Centres at the VC Bird International Airport.

Overseas Tourist Offices

US

610 Fifth Avenue, Suite 311,
New York, NY 10020 ☎ 212-541-
4117; 121 SE 1st Street, Suite
1001, Miami, Florida Fl 33131
☎ 305-381-6762

Canada

60 St Clair Avenue, Toronto,
Ontario M4T 1N5 ☎ 416-961-3085

UK

Antigua House, 15 Thayer Street,
London W1M 5LD
☎ 0237-486-7073

Germany

Thomas strasse 11. D-61348 Bad
Homburg ☎ 49-6172-21504

WEDDINGS

Antigua is becoming an increasingly popular destination for honeymoon couples, and other couples get carried away by the romance of the island and decide to marry while on vacation. If you decide to marry you can enjoy a traditional church ceremony or make your vows on the beach, on a luxury yacht or in a flower-bedecked gazebo by a sparkling hotel pool.

To qualify for a special license you must:

- have a valid passport or birth certificate and ID photo;
- if either party is single, an affidavit must be sworn on Antigua or Barbuda to that affect and that they are free to marry;
- if either party is divorced, a certified copy of the decree absolute must be shown;
- if either party were married and the marriage ended with the death of their partner, a copy of both the marriage and death certificates must be produced;
- if either party is under the age of 18, parental or guardian consent is required. You must be over 15 years old to get married.

There is no waiting time in the country necessary in order to obtain a special license, but both parties must be present at the time of the application which is filled out and signed at the Ministry of Justice and Legal Affairs in Lower Nevis Street, St John's. The petition for a special license costs US$150. There is a US$40 fee to register and the marriage officer's fee is US$50. An ordinary license costs EC $100 and all the above conditions must be met. In addition, one of the parties must have been resident in Antigua or Barbuda for at least 15 days before applying for the license. All marriages must be celebrated in the presence of two or more credible witnesses in addition to the Marriage Officer or Registrar General. Marriage by license can take place anywhere within Antigua and Barbuda providing all the formalities have been complied with and the arrangements accepted by the Registrar General.

Many hotels and resorts offer weddings and honeymoon packages, and have staff experienced in helping with all the formalities and arrangements.

The Registrar General's office is in the High Street, St John's
☎ 462-0609/0409/3929.

And for the Honeymoon…

Several hotels offer specially designed honeymoon packages.

The Admiral's Inn,
Nelson's Dockyard, English
Harbour, Antigua ☎ 460-1027

Antigua Village,
Dickenson Bay ☎ 462-2930

Barrymore Beach Club,
Runaway Bay, Antigua
☎ 462-4101

Blue Waters Beach Hotel,
Soldier's Bay, Antigua
☎ 462-0290

Club Antigua,
Jolly Beach ☎ 462-0061

Copper and Lumber Store Hotel,
Nelson's Dockyard ☎ 460-1058

Falmouth Beach Apartments,
Falmouth Harbour, Antigua
☎ 460-1027

Galley Bay Hotel,
Five Islands, Antigua
☎ 462-0302

Half Moon Bay Club,
Half Moon Bay
☎ 460-4300

Hawksbill Beach Hotel,
Five islands, Antigua
☎ 462-0301

Inn at English Harbour,
English Harbour
☎ 460-1014

Jumby Bay,
Long Island, Antigua
☎ 462-6000

Marina Bay,
Corbinson's Point,
Antigua
☎ 462-3254

Pineapple Beach Club,
Long Bay, Antigua ☎ 463-2006

Rex Halcyon Cove,
Dickenson Bay ☎ 462-025

Sandals Antigua,
Dickenson Bay, Antigua
☎ 462-0267

Siboney Beach Club,
Dickenson Bay ☎ 462-0806

St James's Club,
Marmora Bay, Antigua
☎ 460-5000

Yepton's Beach Resort,
Deep Bay ☎ 462-2520

Sandals Antigua Resort

INDEX

LANDMARK
Publishing Ltd ●●●●

The Caribbean/USA – area guides in this series
'Pack 2 months into 2 weeks'

Virgin Islands
ISBN: 1 901522 03 2
256pp, *UK £12.95 US $15.95*

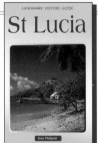

St Lucia
ISBN: 1 901522 28 8
144pp, *UK £6.95 US $13.95*

Bermuda
ISBN: 1 901522 07 5
160pp, *UK £7.95 US $13.95*

Florida: The Keys
ISBN: 1 901522 21 0
160pp, *UK £7.95 US $12.95*

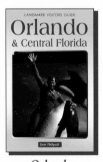

Orlando
ISBN: 1 901522 22 9
256pp, *UK £9.95 US $15.95*

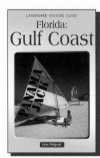

Florida: Gulf Coast
ISBN: 1 901522 01 6
160pp, *UK £7.95 US $12.95*

**See overleaf
For UK & US
ordering addresses**

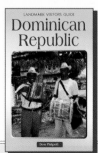

Dominican Republic
ISBN: 1 90152208 3
160pp, Full colour,
UK £7.95 US $12.95

Published in the UK by
Landmark Publishing Ltd,
Waterloo House, 12 Compton, Ashbourne, Derbyshire DE6 1DA England
Tel: 01335 347349 Fax: 01335 347303 e-mail: landmark@clara.net

Published in the USA by
Hunter Publishing Inc
130 Campus Drive, Edison NJ 08818
Tel: (732) 225 1900, (800) 255 0343 Fax: (732) 417 0482
Website: www.hunterpublishing.com

1st Edition
ISBN 1 901 522 02 4

© Don Philpott 2000

The right of Don Philpott as author of this work has been asserted by him in
accordance with the Copyright, Design and Patents Act, 1993.

All rights reserved. No part of this publication may be reproduced, stored in a
retrieval system or transmitted in any form or by any means, electronic,
mechanical, photocopying, recording or otherwise without the prior permission
of Landmark Publishing Ltd.

British Library Cataloguing in Publication Data: a catalogue record for this book
is available from the British Library.

Print: Sun Fung Offset Binding Co Ltd, China
Design: Samantha Witham

Front Cover: The Hawksbill Resort, near St John's
Back cover, top: Nelson's Dockyard
Back cover, bottom: Club Antigua

Picture Credits:
St James's Club: 2,7
Galley Bay Resort: 35
William J Dibble, Magic Hour Concepts: 60
Coco Point Lodge: 61,62
Sandals Antigua Resort: 93
All other photography supplied by the author and P Bathurst

DISCLAIMER
While every care has been taken to ensure that the information in this book
is as accurate as possible at the time of publication, but the publishers
and author accept no responsibility for any loss, injury or inconvenience
sustained by anyone using this book.